CARIBBEAN CRISIS

JAY MALLIN is particularly well equipped to write about Latin America, and especially Cuba and the Caribbean. In 1956, he became a full-time stringer correspondent for *Time*. He covered the entire Cuban revolution (1956–58), contending with intercepted cables, tapped telephones, and threats of personal violence. He made eighteen trips to the battle area, often under assumed names and sometimes posing as an engineer. He was the first to report the presence of Russian troops and missiles in Cuba.

Completely bilingual and raised in Cuba (although born in New York City of American parents), Mallin studied journalism at Florida Southern College in Lakeland, Florida, receiving an A.B. in 1949.

After graduating from college, he took a position on the English-language daily, *The Havana Herald,* and within a short time rose to the position of news editor. At twenty-three, he was one of the youngest editors in Latin America. In 1952 he was one of the first newspapermen to interview General Fulgencio Batista when he seized power.

After two years Mallin left the *Herald* in order to free-lance articles (one of these was on Ernest Hemingway's life in Cuba), as well as to become assistant stringer for *Time* magazine. He also became correspondent for the following services and publications: *New York Post, Chicago Tribune, Miami News, Wall Street Journal, Variety,* Religious News Service, *Business International,* and *Editor & Publisher.*

His book, *Fortress Cuba,* was published in 1965.

Caribbean Crisis

BY

JAY MALLIN

Doubleday & Company, Inc.
Garden City, New York

Library of Congress Catalog Card Number 65–25835
Copyright © 1965 by Jay Mallin
All Rights Reserved
Printed in the United States of America
First Edition

Excerpt from "The Dominican Upheaval" (*Life*, May 28, 1965) by John Bartlow Martin. Copyright © 1965 by John Bartlow Martin. Used with permsision of Harold Ober Associates.

To Caroll
Remembering Havana as we knew it
—and as it will be again one day

Contents

CARIBBEAN CRISIS

Out of the Dominican crucible the twenty American nations must now forge a stronger shield against disaster. The opportunity is here now for a new thrust forward to show the world the way to true international cooperation in the cause of peace and in the struggle to win a better life for all of us.

PRESIDENT LYNDON B. JOHNSON

CHAPTER I

The Background

AMADO GARCIA is a street which runs through a downtown, middle-class section of Santo Domingo, capital of the Dominican Republic. This day the street was littered with debris, spent cartridges, fallen wires and toppled telephone poles, and in the air clung the sweet smell of death and burnt cordite. Amado Garcia had been a battleground in the fierce civil war which was raging in the Dominican capital. In some of the houses that lined the street dead bodies had remained undisturbed for several days, the bodies of men fallen in the war.

Now American Marines and paratroopers had landed in the Dominican Republic. The green-clad men of the 82nd Airborne Division had secured one end of Amado Garcia Street, but at the other end snipers still fired sporadically from two tall buildings.

Crouching and sticking close to the walls, troopers and an officer moved up the street. They jumped small walls, dashed across intersections, stopped and watched. The snipers did not fire—

1

perhaps they had left. Three heavily armed reconnaissance jeeps roared up the street and past the buildings where the snipers had been. No one fired and the jeeps went up a side street.

The infantrymen continued moving forward slowly and cautiously. In the distance, the thumping of grenades and the staccato roar of automatic fire indicated that a fire fight was under way at some point in the city.

The infantrymen were now near the tall buildings, one green, one gray, looming over the end of the street. The three jeeps were returning, swinging around the corner and back onto Amado Garcia.

Suddenly sharp, angry red flames flashed out from the two tall buildings. The jeeps were caught in a devastating crossfire. Several of the American soldiers were hit. One was killed instantly and fell out of the jeep. His buddies leaped out and pushed the body back into the vehicle. The men in the jeeps fired back as the drivers gunned down the street in order to escape the crossfire. The infantrymen also hurriedly retreated.

What had brought American soldiers to the Dominican Republic to fight and die there?

The history of the Dominican Republic has not been a happy one. Its people have known little tranquillity, and in more than thirty-five years they have had only seven months of freely elected government.

The Dominican Republic shares the 30,000-square-mile island of Hispaniola with the equally tragic Haitian nation. Leaving the island for the fourth and last time, Christopher Columbus remarked, "There, in that high and mountainous land, is the land of God." Columbus could not foresee what the future held for Hispaniola (named after Spain), so perhaps this was a permissible error on his part.

First the Spanish dominated the island, and then the French. When the Europeans were finally driven out, the Dominicans were subjugated by their neighbors, the Haitians, who occupied the country for twenty-two brutal years. In 1844, when Haiti was rent by one of its many civil wars, the Dominicans finally achieved independence. Independence brought no peace, however, for the country was torn by twenty-two revolutions during the next seventy years—plus a period (1861–65) when the Spaniards again ran the country. At one point during the Grant administration, the Dominicans actually sought annexation to the United States, but were turned down by Congress.

In 1916, however, the United States sent in the Marines in order to occupy the country and establish order out of political and economic chaos. The Marines remained until 1924, having carried out public works, set up a national police force and in general stabilized the nation. (The United States continued to watch over customs collections until 1941.)

A constitutionally elected government was installed in 1924, and it remained in office until 1930. In March of that year, the Chief of Staff of the

Army, General Rafael Leónidas Trujillo Molina, overthrew the government and launched his own reign, which was to last for thirty-one years. During that period Trujillo ran the Dominican Republic as if it were a feudal estate. He built roads, houses, and hospitals, improved the water supply and raised the literacy rate. Businesses prospered—and so did Trujillo, who built up a personal fortune estimated at $800,000,000. Trujillo and his family owned 65 percent of the country's sugar production, twelve of its sixteen mills and 35 percent of its arable land.

The Dominicans paid an additional price for this rare period of tranquillity: their absolute loss of self-determination. The political opposition was ruthlessly crushed; thousands of political opponents were tortured, murdered or, if they were more fortunate, exiled (even so, Trujillo did not hesitate to send his agents to kill or kidnap opponents living abroad who annoyed him).

Trujillo also became annoyed at Haitian squatters who had drifted across the border in search of better living conditions. In October of 1937 he ordered his Army to eliminate them, and in a thirty-six-hour bloodbath, 15,000 men, women, and children were murdered. One of the officers who directed the slaughter was Lieutenant General Fausto Caamaño, whose son Francisco would one day play an important role in Dominican affairs.

Trujillo's ego knew no limits (he once remarked, "My only regret is that I was born to rule so small a country"). He decreed the "Era of Trujillo," renamed the capital city Ciudad Trujillo, and had the docile Congress bestow on him the titles of Generalissimo of the Armed Forces, Benefactor of the Fatherland, Restorer of Financial Independence, Chief Protector of the Working Class, Genius of Peace, and First Journalist of the Republic. (Trujillo, needless to say, also ran the country's press.) Trujillo twice made his brother President, and one of Trujillo's sons was made a colonel in the Army— at the age of five.

Trujillo agents carried out an unsuccessful attempt in June of 1960 to assassinate Venezuelan President Rómulo Betancourt, a Trujillo foe, and for this the Organization of American States, in August 1960, roundly condemned the Dominican tyrant and asked its member nations to impose economic and diplomatic sanctions. The United States and several Latin American nations broke diplomatic relations and cut off commerce with the Dominican Republic.

In May 1961, Generalissimo Trujillo was ambushed and assassinated while traveling on a lonely road outside Ciudad Trujillo. One of the men who participated in the assassination was a former official, Antonio Imbert Barreras, and he also would one day play an important role in Dominican affairs.

A period of turbulence followed Trujillo's death, with the country beset by riots, strikes, attempted coups, and Communist agitation. President Joaquín Balaguer continued to rule for a while, backed by Trujillo's son, Rafael, Jr., commander of the armed forces. Then a seven-man Council of State took over, and the last vestiges of the Trujillo regime were eliminated from the government.

In December of 1962, general elections were held, with eight political parties participating. The two main parties were the Unión Cívica Nacional, composed of professional and middle-class elements, and the Partido Revolucionario Dominicano, which was left of center. The U.C.N.'s presidential candidate was Viriato Fiallo, an anti-Trujillo physician. The P.R.D. candidate was Juan Bosch, author, intellectual, and long-time exile. Bosch won the election, receiving almost 59 percent of the ballots that were cast (Fiallo received 30 percent).

In February of 1963, Bosch was inaugurated as the Dominican Republic's first freely elected President since 1924. It was not long, however, before Bosch began to display an acute case of a type of blindness which afflicts some leftist, ivory-tower politicians. He permitted a rapid expansion of Communist activities and the infiltration of Communists and Communist sympathizers into the ranks of the government. Bosch was beset by domestic difficulties, particularly economic ills inherited from the Trujillo regime, and he felt that if he avoided a showdown with the Communists, they would cause him no trouble, of which he already had a goodly amount.

Having lived in exile for twenty-four years, Bosch had had little administrative experience. He had bright plans for his country, including an agrarian reform program, but he was hampered by his own lack of practical ability. Even so, he was fearful of delegating authority, and in his efforts to run every aspect of the Dominican government, he often saw as many as forty people in a fourteen-hour day—and then took work home. On one occasion he dismissed a Cabinet officer and two trusted associates merely because he suspected them of improper practices.

Unrest grew and the general situation deteriorated. The economy worsened; unemployment grew; private capital was frightened away. Bosch moved toward authoritarianism: pressures on the opposition press, establishment of a militia, setting up of "vigilance committees." All of these moves were distinctly reminiscent of the steps taken by Fidel Castro in Cuba when he was setting up his Communist dictatorship.

In May of 1963, Opposition Leader Fiallo sent Bosch an open letter warning him that "the Communist danger in our country is evident and gains impetus from day to day." Fiallo specifically mentioned the vigilance committees, the use of schools for "indoctrination," the putting of Communists "in key places," and even the utilization of government buildings by Communist speechmakers.

Peter Nehemkis, a U.S. lawyer who was appointed by the O.A.S. to be a member of the inter-American commission which monitored the 1962 Dominican elections, subsequently provided a telling description of Bosch in his book *Latin America —Myth and Reality*:

"As the Greek tragic hero is powerless to resist

7

his fate, Bosch, too, was caught in a web of doom. He had a premonition of the impending catastrophe. Shortly after taking office he remarked to a colleague that he felt as if he were the protagonist in a Greek morality play. Bosch assumed the presidency in an environment poisoned by conspiracy. Life under Trujillo had been a perpetual conspiracy. Trujillo's murder was planned and executed by a conspiracy. . . .

"[Bosch] could not tolerate criticism. He was unable to delegate authority. He offended old and tried friends. He preached democracy but practiced *caudillismo*. He dismissed the members of the Electoral Board, the body that made his own election possible, and replaced them with political henchmen. He packed the judiciary with party followers, thus destroying its independence. Bosch used his own party as a vehicle to accomplish the 'dirty work' of carrying out controversial Leftist reforms. At the same time, he was engaged in liquidating his own party because at heart he was a *caudillo* who could not tolerate the political discipline of party organization. It is significant that at the moment when his downfall was imminent, his own party did not rise to defend him."

In July 1963, the Dominican Episcopate issued a statement in which the bishops declared that they "could not conceal their profound concern in the face of the bitter reality of the moment in which Dominican society is living, of uncertainty and of a lack of confidence . . ." In addition the bishops asserted, "The political developments in the country which are occurring have not succeeded in establishing the reign of true peace . . . Nor can it be said that there is a Dominican home where full tranquillity is enjoyed." The bishops bluntly assailed "the Communist ideologies which ignore respect for man, which consider man to be a simple gear of the machinery of the state . . ."

On September 20 a general strike was launched throughout the country. Unable to break the strike, the Bosch regime began to topple. The *coup d'grace* was delivered by the armed forces, who sent Bosch off into exile. On September 25 Army, Navy, and Air Force leaders issued a "communiqué to the people" announcing that the Bosch government had been deposed and that "the Communist doctrine, Marxist-Leninist, Castroite, or whatever it is called," was now outlawed, as well as the political parties that followed this ideology.

One of the leaders in the military revolt was Colonel (later General) Elías Wessin y Wessin, head of the armed forces training center. The Dominican Air Force has troops and tanks, as well as planes, and by using these Wessin emerged as a new strong man.

A civilian triumvirate was set up, whose original three members were eventually replaced by two others, although the two-man group continued to be called "the Triumvirate." The leader of the duo—and thus the *de facto* President of the country—was Donald Reid Cabral, a well-to-do automobile dealer of partially Scotch descent. Reid launched an austerity program, tried to crack down on military graft, planned to hold free elections.

But once again there was unrest in the land. A long drought left the cities almost waterless, hampered the farmers in growing their crops, frayed tempers everywhere. Much of the land turned into red dust. Some of the military resented Reid's reform efforts; others, leaning left, yearned for the return of Bosch. Tourism was down, exports were off, the Dominican peso fell in value.

A conspiracy evolved and grew, involving both military and civilian elements. Bosch, despite his status as a political asylee in Puerto Rico, plotted with his followers, and couriers shuttled back and forth between San Juan and the Dominican Republic. Considerable numbers of Dominicans trained in Cuba began slipping across the Windward Passage and returning to their homeland.

Reid was fully aware that a conspiracy was under way. He later stated: "In the past few months the political parties directed by the Communists had been working on the military, saying it was 'unbelievable that a civilian could control them.' The principal place where the coup was going on was at the February 27 Army Training School on the Duarte Highway to Santiago. Since I didn't want bloodshed, I went there on April 19 with Army Chief of Staff General Marcos Rivera Cuesta and my military aide on the pretense of inspecting the school. This would give them a chance to take me prisoner, and bloodshed would be avoided. But they didn't do anything."

Early in the morning of April 24, however, General Rivera Cuesta returned to the February 27 encampment with the intention of dismissing four Army officers. Instead, he was taken prisoner by the conspirators. These then went to Rivera Cuesta's headquarters and broke into his desk, where they found the names of other officers who were suspect by the government. These officers were alerted, and a radio station was called and informed that a revolt had begun.

The tragic events which would soon lead to the landing of American troops in the Dominican Republic for the first time in forty-one years were now under way.

CHAPTER II

The Rebels

On Saturday, April 24, at about 2:30 P.M., three Army sergeants and fifteen civilians charged into Radio Santo Domingo and seized the station. They announced a "triumphant revolution to restore Juan Bosch to the presidency," and they declared, "Constitutional forces are on the move against the usurpers."

The rebel announcement sent crowds swirling into the streets, where agitators whipped them into a frenzy. Mobs invaded a fire station and stole the engines, which they drove wildly through the streets, sirens howling. Truckloads of Bosch followers chanted: "Bosch! Bosch! *Viva* Bosch!" and displayed "Constitution with Bosch" signs.

Important Army units, troops at the February 27 and August 16 encampments, rebelled and joined the revolt.

Even so, loyal forces recaptured Radio Santo Domingo, and at around 7 P.M., President Reid went on the air to announce that the country was

13

quiet and that the greater part of the armed forces were still loyal to the government.

During the early morning hours of the following morning, the rebel military units moved out of their encampments and into the city.

The rebel movement grew rapidly, but the only thing the rebels were agreed upon, at this early stage, was that no one was in favor of Reid remaining in office. Reid asked General Wessin for support, but Wessin refused to give it. Reid had no alternative but to resign, and he and the other member of the "triumvirate," Ramón Cáceres Troncoso, did so. Reid went into hiding at a friend's house.

The military, while agreeing that Reid had to go, could not agree on what to replace him with. Some (including Wessin) favored establishment of a military junta. Others urged the return of ex-President Balaguer. And still others sought to have Bosch reinstalled as President.

The pro-Bosch group, supported by P.R.D. officials, gained the upper hand, and on April 25 they announced that a pro-Bosch man, José Rafael Molina Ureña, former speaker of the Chamber of Deputies, had been named "Provisional Constitutional President." In San Juan, Bosch stated that he would go to Santo Domingo "just as soon as the Air Force sends a plane for me." (A photographer who got a look into Bosch's bedroom spotted a ouija board there.)

A reign of terror began sweeping over Santo Domingo. On Sunday rebel Army men drove four truckloads of weapons into the Ciudad Nueva, a low-cost housing area in the southeast section of the city, and they distributed the arms to all takers: everything from small arms to bazookas and .50-calibre machine guns. Some of the weapons were used to establish strongpoints; others were taken by bands of uncontrolled *"tigres"* (tigers), hoodlums who looted stores and fired indiscriminately. The police, last vestige of governmental authority, became the special targets of the rebels. The rebel radio screamed: "Kill a policeman! Kill a policeman!" A university student belonging to the pro-Castro June 14 Movement boasted: "We joined this thing in the beginning just so we could kill those bastards. And, *hombre*, we wipe them out very good!" One police station, at Villa Consuelo, was surrounded and attacked by armed civilians. Within thirty minutes the station had been overrun, and the police who were caught inside were shot on the spot. Others who managed to get out, but were pursued and captured, were also killed.

The rebels had retaken Radio Santo Domingo and Santo Domingo Television and were using these to transmit messages and to broadcast propaganda. Members of the June 14 Movement served as announcers, and a parade of rebels—civilians as well as military—voiced the rebel line, denounced the "oligarchies" and yelled for Bosch. One teen-age girl announced, "I'm going out to die for my country."

"President" Molina Ureña issued a statement, declaring, "As president of the Constitutional Congress of the republic, I formally proclaim that the 1963 Constitution is in full effect and a truly democratic state is restored in the Dominican Republic, and I provisionally assume the presidency of the Dominican Republic until the return to his native land of Prof. Juan Bosch, the constitutional President."

But the rebels, despite what they might think, had not won, and Bosch was not returning—at least not yet. On April 26 Wessin made his first major move. He ordered his F-51s to strafe the National (Presidential) Palace and the western approaches to the strategic Duarte Bridge. San Isidro lies to the east of Santo Domingo, across from the Ozama River. Wessin controlled the area east of the bridge and the river; the rebels held most of the western bank. They had barricaded the bridge in an effort to stop any attack by Wessin's tanks and troops across the river. Now the F-51s were attacking in an effort to soften up the rebel positions prior to an assault by Wessin's land forces. (Navy forces also joined the fray, and warships offshore shelled the Palace.)

The air attacks drove the rebels into new frenzies. The rebel radio broadcast the addresses of relatives of the fliers and ordered, "Find the pilots' families and bring them to us." Frightened wives and children of the airmen were dragged before the television cameras. An announcer warned: "We are going to hold them at the bridge. If you strafe there, you kill them." (One pilot defected and flew his plane to Puerto Rico.)

Santo Domingo Radio broadcast a call to the people: "Attention! Attention! The air force is bombing the Duarte Bridge, and from the other side of the Duarte Bridge . . . the tanks are blockading the road and are shooting at the city. They are doing this, Dominicans, so that you will not go out in the streets to defend your constitutionality. Do not be afraid. Get out on the streets, Dominican people, to defend your constitutionality. Swarm into the streets of the capital!"

Wessin's troops crossed the bridge, but they were unable to effect any sizable penetration into the rebel area. Nevertheless, the fact that Wessin was still firmly in control of his forces, and the fact that he could and was launching air attacks, demoralized a portion of the rebel leadership. Dozens fled into asylum in foreign embassies; "President" Molina quit at around 1:30 A.M. on April 28 and obtained asylum in the Colombian Embassy. The defectors were frightened by the growing bloodshed, by the uncontrolled mobs and by the fact that the Communists seemed to be taking over the rebel movement. A high official of Bosch's own party broadcast an appeal over the San Isidro radio station: "I beg all to lay down their arms, turning them in to the nearest military post, because this is no longer a fight between political parties."

The mobs turned their wrath hither and yon. They sacked a new Pepsi-Cola plant (and used the bottles to make Molotov cocktails), attacked Reid's auto agency, seized the offices of anti-Bosch newspapers and sacked the offices of anti-Communist political parties. The grounds of the embassy of El Salvador were violated by armed men; shots were fired at the Argentinean, Ecuadorean and other embassies. The Guatemalan ambassador was threatened by a mob that demanded that they be allowed to search the embassy for an anti-Bosch radio commentator they were hunting. "This is collective madness," U.S. Ambassador Tapley Bennett declared.

The U.S. Embassy was gathering Americans and other foreigners at the Embajador Hotel on the outskirts of town, preparatory to evacuation. A group of rebels suddenly appeared, most of them teenagers, and they began waving their guns and terrorizing the foreigners, firing their automatic weapons over the heads of the terrified group. An American housewife commented bitterly, "Those brats just seemed to delight in terrorizing us."

The refugees who were evacuated from Santo Domingo told of the chaos and horrors they had witnessed. A Mexican related: "I was about to have lunch when I first heard of the trouble. There was machine-gun fire throughout the city. I spent several days with friends in Santo Domingo, a period in my life which I will never forget. The thing got worse and worse and worse. Planes began to bomb the city, and also the ships started shelling it. It was fearful."

Another refugee recalled: "On April 25, at about 7:30 A.M., when I arrived by car at the corner of the Parque Independencia and Avenida Independencia, a couple of civilians armed with machine guns ordered me to stop, and a third civilian ordered me back. But I couldn't go in reverse because a car was directly behind me. I saw a man get out who looked like a Spaniard, about 21 or 22 years old. It seemed he was the one the civilians were awaiting in order to go on with the shooting that I was about to witness.

"At the corner of the park there was a group of about seventy men armed with machine guns, and I also saw sixteen or seventeen men naked from the waist up, without shoes. To me they looked like policemen because of the color of their trousers, and their type of belts identified them as such. They were desperate and begged for mercy. The Spaniard ordered the execution immediately. Ten men were selected from the seventy to be the firing squad. I couldn't make myself look at the men but turned my gaze upon the Spaniard who ordered the cold-blooded execution of the men. The executed men had been tied together by their waists, and when they were machine-gunned, their bodies slumped forward but they did not fall to the ground."

As the civil war continued unabated, a number of changes occurred in the upper governmental structures of the two sides. A three-man military junta (Army, Navy, and Air Force) was set up at San Isidro, but this was later replaced by a five-man (military and civilian) "Government of National Reconstruction." President of the new ruling body was General Imbert, survivor of the Trujillo assassination (for which he was rewarded with the rank of brigadier general, although he had not previously been in the Army). The government set itself up in a congressional building, and after being sworn in in the Senate chamber, Imbert promised to work for peace, national unity, economic reconstruction, and "progressive democracy."

On the rebel side, a curious figure emerged as the new leader. He was Colonel Francisco Alberto Caamaño Deñó. Francisco was the son of Lieutenant General Fausto Caamaño, a former boss of Trujillo's secret police, organizer of the "Cuarenta Dos" (the "Forty-two")—a strongarm gang, and one-time chief of Trujillo's Air Force, until he was replaced in 1954 by Trujillo's pet son, Ramfis.

Francisco was born in the Dominican Republic around 1933, and he entered the Trujillo Navy as a cadet in 1950. He was promoted regularly due to his father's influence.

In 1954, Caamaño was transferred to the Dominican Marines with the rank of captain. He was given training at American Marine bases in the United States, but later Trujillo abolished the Dominican Marines, and Caamaño became an Army captain.

In 1959, Caamaño participated in the extermination of the June 14 invasion by Castro-trained Dominicans, and he received a decoration from Trujillo.

After Trujillo was assassinated, Caamaño was transferred to the National Police, where he rose to the rank of colonel. In December 1962, Caamaño commanded police and troops who shot up a rebellious religious sect in Palma Sola, near the Haitian border. Most members of the sect appear to have been Haitian.

In his book, *Crisis of Democracy*, Juan Bosch described the Palma Sola affair as "genocide."

Nevertheless, Caamaño commanded the elite police unit, the "Cascos Blancos" (white helmets), during Bosch's regime.

Caamaño participated in Bosch's overthrow, and later he plotted to oust his chief, National Police Commander General Belisario Beguerro. The plot failed, and President Reid removed Caamaño from the police and tried to send him off as consul general in Kingston, Jamaica.

Caamaño refused to go and asked to be allowed back into the armed forces. Reid relented, and Caamaño was assigned to the Air Force.

When the conspiracy began brewing, Caamaño warned Reid of the plot. He then engaged in some nimble footwork: on April 24 he helped the rebels with radio propaganda; on April 25 he ducked into the Salvadorean Embassy and asked for asylum; then he ducked out again and returned to the rebels. On May 4 he was proclaimed "Constitutionalist President" by the rebels.

How did Caamaño rise so rapidly? Clearly he suited a purpose for the rebels, Communist as well as non-Communist. He was ambitious, he could be handled, and he could not be labeled as a Communist because clearly he was not one—at least not yet. In a word, he served as a semi-respectable "front" for the rebels, and as such he was utilized to the utmost, particularly in interviews and at press conferences with American correspondents. He would heatedly deny that he was Communist or that the rebel movement was Communist—the rebels, he would say, were fighting for honest and constitutional government.

On May 11, Caamaño delivered an address over Radio Santo Domingo, declaring: "I say that side by side with the Dominicans, I will wage the battle we have undertaken without vacillation and without halfway measures until we gain total success. . . . Despite the tremendous propaganda by United States publicity organs based on the erratic or ill-intentioned reports by Ambassador Bennett, our revolutionary movement is eminently democratic. . . . Only the Constitutionalist Government is legitimate, for it alone has emanated from the will of the Dominicans. . . ."

The words sounded fine: Caamaño was serving his deceptive purpose. But even so, his talk of "liberty, justice, economic progress and social security" did not obscure the arson, the pillaging, the wanton killing—all carried out in the name of "constitutionality." Castro, in Cuba, had once used a pretty word, too. It was "humanism."

CHAPTER III

The GIs

"FOR TWO DAYS American forces have been in Santo Domingo in an effort to protect the lives of Americans and the nationals of other countries in the face of increasing violence and disorder. With the assistance of these American forces, over 2,400 Americans and other nationals have been evacuated from the Dominican Republic. We took this step when, and only when, we were officially notified by police and military officials of the Dominican Republic that they were no longer in a position to guarantee the safety of American and foreign nationals and to preserve law and order. In the last twenty-four hours violence and disorder have increased."

Thus spoke President Lyndon B. Johnson to the nation on the night of April 30. The situation in Santo Domingo had indeed deteriorated rapidly since the rebellion had broken out. Hooligans were sacking stores, mobs roamed the streets screaming, *"Paredón! Paredón!"* ("To the wall! To the wall!"), foreign embassies were attacked, shooting was widespread and casualty tolls were rising into the thousands. Bodies were disposed of by fire, and harried doctors operated by flashlight and without anesthetics. Santo Domingo was without water, without power, without food and without the slightest semblance of law and order.

U.S. Ambassador W. Tapley Bennett, Jr., had been in the States when the revolt broke out. He was rushed back to his embassy in Santo Domingo by jet and helicopter and immediately plunged into the situation. Among others, he twice conferred with rebel leaders, including Colonel Caamaño. Primarily through the efforts of the Papal Nuncio, Monsignor Emanuelle Clarizio, a ceasefire was agreed to by the rebels and the government, but the situation was too anarchic, and as a result there was no real letup in the firing.

Trapped amidst the chaos and bloodletting, the Americans in Santo Domingo were in acute danger. The peril was dramatically underscored by the incident at the Embajador Hotel, when the rebels fired over the heads of the group of helpless men. This incident helped convince Ambassador Bennett that U.S. forces were needed to protect American lives.

In Washington, President Johnson was conferring with his top aides, including Secretary of State Dean Rusk, Defense Secretary Robert McNamara, and other aides. The reports from Santo Domingo were becoming more alarming. Not only were American citizens, as well as other foreign nationals, in serious danger, but there were also growing indications of Communist participation in the rebellion.

Orders were flashed to Task Force 124, including the aircraft carrier *Boxer*, to speed to Santo Domingo. Other orders to Fort Bragg, North Carolina, started the 82nd Airborne Division winging south. President Johnson went on television to announce: "The United States Government has been informed by military authorities in the Dominican Republic that American lives are in danger. These authorities are no longer able to guarantee their safety and they have reported that the assistance of military personnel is now needed for that purpose. I have ordered the Secretary of Defense to put the necessary American troops ashore in order to give protection to hundreds of Americans who are still in the Dominican Republic and to escort them safely back to this country. This same assistance will be available to the nationals of other countries, some of whom have already asked for our help."

The decision to send American troops into a Latin American country was not an easy one to make. Not since 1927, when Marines landed in Nicaragua, had the United States intervened in a Hemisphere country. Strict non-intervention had become a cornerstone of U.S. policy in Latin America. Now, however, the situation in Santo Domingo demanded a new and immediate decision. President Johnson explained that decision in an address on May 2:

"Ambassador Bennett, who is one of our most experienced Foreign Service officers . . . [stated in a cable] that only an immediate landing of American forces could safeguard and protect the lives of thousands of Americans and thousands of other citizens of some thirty other countries. Ambassador Bennett urged your President to order an immediate landing.

"In this situation, hesitation and vacillation could mean death for many of our people, as well as many of the citizens of other lands.

"I thought that we could not, and we did not, hesitate. Our forces, American forces, were ordered in immediately to protect American lives. They have done that. They have attacked no one, and although some of our servicemen gave their lives, not a single American civilian and the civilian of any other nation, as a result of this protection, lost their lives."

During the early evening of Wednesday, April 28, the first Marines landed in Santo Domingo. Elements of the 3rd Battalion, 6th Marine Regiment, climbed into helicopters aboard the *Boxer* and were flown to the disused polo field adjoining the Embajador Hotel. The Marines seized the field, took over the hotel, dug in and set up a defensive perimeter. A platoon was sent to defend the U.S. Embassy, a little over a mile away.

The Marines met rebel resistance. Snipers fired at them near the hotel, and at the embassy two Marines were killed by machine-gun fire. These were the first American casualties. There would be more.

At 2 A.M. on April 30, the first elements of two battalions of the 82nd Airborne arrived at the San

[1] A young Dominican boy ducks behind a U.S. Army medical aid vehicle as rebel sniper fire is heard near the Colegio Maria Auxiliador hospital in Santo Domingo.

[2] A U.S. soldier distributes rations of food to citizens of Santo Domingo.

[3] *top left*, Three-year-old Santa Justina displays a dress she received from U.S. troops stationed in the Dominican Republic. Such clothing and toys were collected in the United States by wives of servicemen.

[4] *lower right*, A young Dominican boy admires the helmet and body armor jacket of a U.S. marine.

[5] U.S. troops share some of their food rations with young Dominican boys.

Isidro air base. Tentative plans had called for the men to parachute in, but later it was deemed safe enough to bring the paratroopers in their C-124 and C-130 transport planes. The troopers occupied a portion of the airfield and also the road from the airfield leading to the Duarte Bridge. The troops took over a small area on the western side of the bridge, so that the bridge would also be secure.

In addition to the first 405 Marines that landed, an additional 1200 were flown in as re-enforcements. The Marines fanned out and established an "International Safety Zone," an area of nine square miles which included the Embajador, the U.S. Embassy and several other embassies.

The evacuation of Americans and nationals of other countries proceeded rapidly. Brown helicopters whirled back and forth between evacuation points and the American ships offshore, carrying approximately 2000 Americans and some 2500 Europeans and Latin Americans to safety. Occasionally the helicopters drew fire from rebel snipers.

Although a number of Latin American countries had been critical of the U.S. move into the Dominican Republic, those of their citizens who were taken to safety by the American forces were not reticent in expressing their gratitude. A Peruvian university professor, Rafael Reategui, stated: "I do not have words to express how grateful we are to the North American authorities for having evacuated us. The evacuation could not have been more opportune, and thanks to that measure, we are here safe and sound." An Argentine engineer, Lorenzo Dotta, stated: "There, there is no respect for the life of any human being, and only the presence of the Marines was a guarantee of security." The Salvadorean ambassador to the Dominican Republic, Luis Roberto Flores, publicly expressed his "most sincere gratitude to the United States government and people for having saved all the elements of the Salvadorean colony in the Dominican Republic."

Once the evacuation had been completed, it was still evident that to withdraw the American forces would be folly. Although there was still sporadic fighting, especially sniping, it was clear that the presence of the U.S. troops had restored a semblance of order to the city. Their withdrawal would plunge the city back into chaos—a chaos in which the trained, disciplined Communist apparatus might well emerge with the upper hand. The United States could not abandon the Dominican Republic.

On May 5 I filed the following dispatch from Santo Domingo to *Life* magazine: "The first American forces that landed were the Marines, who set up strongpoints at the U.S. Embassy and at the Hotel Embajador. Shortly afterwards came the paratroopers, who established themselves at the San Isidro air base and also secured the road from San Isidro to the Duarte Bridge.

"Early this week the Marines and the paratroopers drove toward each other and effected a junction. A corridor—'Battle Alley'—was thus established all the way between San Isidro and the embassy and Embajador. The military prefer to call it a 'line of communications,' and it is just that. Now troops and equipment that land at San Isidro can be brought by road to the International Safety Zone, and will not have to be carried by helicopter, as was previously the case.

"The corridor consists primarily of a single road. At each intersection leading into it, barricades of debris, tree branches, barbed wire and demolished vehicles have been set up. A heavy concentration of U.S. troops and Marines guard the corridor, armed with weapons ranging from M-14 rifles to fifty-two-ton tanks.

"The Americans must frequently leap behind cover when rebel snipers open up from nearby buildings. The U.S. troops are under tight firing discipline: they do not fire unless they are fired at first. Even then, the larger weapons cannot be fired without the approval of unit commanders.

"On some of the walls can be seen old, scrawled signs: 'Yankees, get out of Viet Nam' and 'Yankees go home.' The Yankees ignore the signs and haven't even bothered to paint them over.

"Two or three intersections have been kept open on the corridor. All civilian vehicles, however, are carefully searched. Military policemen direct the traffic, evidently unconcerned over the danger of sniper fire.

"The massive U.S. military buildup continues. Offshore lies a fleet of twenty-four warships, including the carriers *Boxer* and *Okinawa*. The biggest airlift since the Berlin blockade is under way, with huge planes bringing thousands of troops and more

29

than 30,000,000 pounds of supplies into San Isidro. The planes are landing at an average rate of one every six minutes.

"A week after the first Marines landed, over 14,-000 troops (Marines, paratroopers, Special Forces, Seabees, a "cavalry" unit) are now on the island, and more are arriving. The casualty toll is also rising, and so far six Americans have died and 48 have been wounded. Two are listed as 'missing.' No one knows how many Dominicans have died, but the figure is estimated in the thousands."

The presence of the American soldiers infuriated the rebels. They continually sniped at them, and sometimes launched even heavier barrages. On several occasions U.S. vehicle drivers got lost and inadvertently wandered into areas held by the rebels, who then opened fire, killing several Marines and paratroopers in this way.

Rebel radio stations continuously and viciously assailed the Americans, often inciting Dominicans to fire at them. Radio Constitución broadcast: "The North Americans are continuing to advance and expand the so-called neutral zone. The Yankees say they have received permission from the Dominican authorities. They do not specify that by authorities they mean the Wessin gang, which has called them in as re-enforcements while they retreat and avoid the defeat the Dominican people are dealing them.

"It is untrue that an agreement has been made to make the so-called neutral zone as broad as possible. The invaders are seeking to steal ground from the people, to weaken the position of the Constitutionalists and gain land for Wessin and his assassins.

"All the people should receive the Yankee invaders as enemies. All the people should fire on the Yankees who are outside the neutral zone. All the people should keep watch on the Yankees and guard against their crafty movements.

"Dominica yes! Yankees no! Out with the Yankees!"

A steady propaganda barrage was maintained against the U.S. forces. On one occasion Radio Constitución called on Dominicans to "drive out the Yankee raiders who commit rape and murder." Radio Santo Domingo on May 11 broadcast the following:

"U.S. Marines have attacked several homes in Santo Domingo, inflicting wounds, destroying property and sowing fear. The Marines have used machine guns, grenades and other weapons against the people of Santo Domingo. The U.S. Government will be sued for damages. The Marines ransacked homes and took several prisoners, whom they tied and left in the sun. Some of the prisoners were tied and exhibited in public . . . The people of Santo Domingo must defend their rights."

The rebels attempted to take their hate campaign to the United Nations. Their "foreign minister," Jottin Cury, sent a letter to Secretary General U Thant charging that U.S. troops "are carrying out abuses against the civilian population, inhumane treatment of prisoners, violation of the principles of human rights . . . arbitrary arrests, violation of homes, destruction of private property."

Despite the rebel charges, no proof of the alleged American atrocities was to be found. There were some two hundred newsmen in Santo Domingo, Americans as well as correspondents from Asia, Europe, and Latin America, and they were permitted freedom of movement throughout the U.S. zone. None discovered misbehavior on the part of the U.S. soldiers, and one correspondent commented, "They are a lot better behaved than the GIs in World War II."

The American troops were subjected to constant harassment by the rebel snipers. The following is an actual military record for a typical day (May 11):

Time	Incident
845	One round fired into LOC (line of communication). No fire returned.
1135	Single sniper round fired into ISZ (international safety zone). No fire returned.
1340	Fourteen rounds fired vicinity east side of river. Type of weapons unknown. Fire returned.
1430	Small arms firing into San Souci Beach area. Fire returned.
1510	Six rounds from small calibre weapons fired vicinity east side of river. Fire returned.
1515	One round from .22-calibre weapon fired into LOC. No fire returned.
1530	ISZ attacked by twenty rebels, eighteen with small arms, two with bazookas. Fire returned.
1635	Twenty rounds fired from automatic and small arms weapons vicinity east side of river. No fire returned.

1801	Rounds fired from small arms and machine guns vicinity east side of river. Fire returned.
1815	Thirty-five rounds from automatic and semi-automatic weapons fired into LOC. Weapons believed to have silencers; could not hear firing. Fire returned.
1815	Approximately twenty-five rounds sniper small arms fire received in ISZ. Fire returned.
1830	One round fired into company area east of Ozama Bridge. No fire returned.
1845	Three rounds fired from tracer rifle into LOC. No fire returned. One round fired from small calibre rifle into LOC at another point. No fire returned.
2010	Large volume of rebel small arms fire received in ISZ. Fire returned.
2310	Command post in ISZ received small arms and automatic weapons fire. Fire returned.
2315	Small arms fire received in command post west of polo grounds. No fire returned.

As can be seen, not even the ISZ—the International Safety Zone—was entirely safe. Snipers might strike at any place, and for soldiers sitting and waiting in their foxholes or at checkpoints, this could be a particularly trying type of warfare.

And in some ways, it was a strange war, too. The American troops were under orders to remain strictly neutral, but there were rebels shooting at them and wounding them and killing them. The

33

troops, trained in modern warfare of mobility, were largely confined to static positions, and sometimes they felt like wooden ducks in the shooting gallery of a nickel arcade. They were not allowed to fire unless fired upon, and on one occasion they had to remain passive while they saw rebels lifting a machine-gun piece by piece to a rooftop, and then assembling it, and then firing with it. Finally, at this point, an American officer later commented dryly, "We dismantled it." It was a strange war in other ways, also. The United Press International carried the following dispatch from one of its correspondents:

SANTO DOMINGO—It was, as the Marine said, a hell of a way to fight a war.

For one thing, there were all these Dominican civilians sitting on their front porches watching.

And then there was the TV cameraman filming Sgt. Dennis Lamoreaux busily squeezing off rounds with his M-14 rifle at a rebel who had climbed a tree on a jetty sticking out in the Caribbean.

The Third Platoon of Dog Company deployed, but it is doubtful that the Marines ever learned to do it "that way" back at Camp Lejeune.

So when shots began whistling toward the Third Platoon from the direction of the jetty, the lieutenant said that it was O.K. to shoot. Sgt. Lamoreaux's third or fourth shot brought something that looked a lot like a man toppling out of the tree.

The sergeant lit a cigarette . . .

War at Checkpoint Dallas sometimes seems unreal. A Marine can stand around the corner and buy a cold beer at the grocery store and think it over. Or he can try out his high school Spanish on

34

the Dominican girls who stop by to say a lot of things that don't sound like "Yankee go home."

That's the way it was yesterday at Checkpoint Dallas. As the Marine said, it was a hell of a way to fight a war.

The American soldiers, however, did more than wait for sniper fire and then return it. They launched an extensive humanitarian program to help the citizens of the stricken city. Technicians were able to get the power plant back into operation, and the city had electricity once again. Civilian work crews were organized to unload relief supplies and to clean up accumulations of garbage and debris. Food, water, and medical supplies were distributed to hospitals, and military field hospitals treated civilian sick and wounded. Dominican truckers were provided with scarce gasoline so that they could bring rice into the city from the interior of the country.

A military patrol discovered a 150-bed hospital nearly full of patients, but lacking electric power and clean bedding, and short of food, water and medical supplies. A list of needed supplies was obtained from the physician in charge and an urgent request went to an Army supply center in the United States. A 100-man labor force was recruited to improve sanitary conditions, and a 3000-gallon water tank containing pure water was installed. The badly needed supplies began to arrive.

Food distribution points were set up in the corridor and in the safety zone, and civilians lined up to receive rice, beans, flour, cornmeal, cooking oil, and

35

powdered milk. No distinction was made as to whether the civilians came from the rebel or the loyalist zones—all were given supplies by the American soldiers. Catholic and Protestant clergymen assisted in the distribution. One woman, carrying an infant on an arm and leading another child by the hand, said she had walked five miles to the distribution point. Some women were accompanied by six or more children.

The people stood in line with every type of container: tin cans, gunnysacks, even their hats. One youngster was observed dashing with his hands cupped in order to minimize his loss of rice. The Americans solved this problem, too. They requested and received from the United States one million paper bags, in which the food could be given away.

Many American soldiers carried out their own private food distribution. Barefoot Dominican youngsters, awed but friendly, would cluster around, and often they would share the soldiers' fare: C rations.

CHAPTER IV

The Communists

CUBAN DICTATOR Fidel Castro Ruz had been in power only three months when he declared, "The Caribbean is ours," and ever since then he has been working hard to make that statement come true.

Castro's primary target in the Caribbean has been the Dominican Republic, which, because of its unstable condition, has been particularly susceptible to subversion. The 1965 rebellion marked the third major effort by Castro to subvert that country.

The first attempt was described in my book *Fortress Cuba*: "Late in the afternoon of June 14, 1959, soon after Castro had solidified his power in Cuba, eighty men wearing olive-green uniforms boarded a gray C-46 at an airfield near Antilla, in the northern part of Cuba's Oriente Province. The plane bore Dominican markings. The men wore armbands which displayed a red and blue shield and the letters 'UPD,' representing the *Union Patriotica Dominicana*, a Dominican exile group. Loaded aboard the plane were food and ammunition sufficient for fifteen days, and the men carried FN Belgian rifles,

Garands, M-1s, bazookas and machine guns. . . . In command of the group of men was Enrique Jimenes Moya, a Red-tinged Dominican exile who had served as a captain with Castro's guerrillas.

"The plane took off and headed eastward, holding close to the route and timetable of a regular Delta Airlines' flight in order to avoid radar detection. Two hours later, the C-46 landed at an airfield outside Constanza, a town of three thousand people set in the Dominican Republic's Central Mountain Range. The expeditionaries piled out of the plane and quickly overcame the small handful of surprised soldiers on guard at the field. They captured several vehicles and used these to race into town, where they attacked a garrison of about fifteen men, killing or wounding most of them. Other troops, stationed outside of town, headed toward Constanza, but were ambushed by the rebels. Following this fight, the rebels retired into the surrounding hills."

Two hundred additional rebels who had sailed from Cuba on June 13 in two converted yachts carried out landings at two points on the northwest Dominican troops. The regular Dominican military were, however, the best in the Caribbean at that time, and Dictator Trujillo soon had them in determined pursuit of the rebels. Within weeks all of the rebels were killed or captured, and Castro's first effort to subvert the Dominican Republic had failed.

The second major attempt was made in 1963. A pro-Castro political party had been formed, the *Agrupación Politica Catorce de Junio* (June 14th Political Group, named after the 1959 expedition).

The June 14th sent a group of approximately twenty-five men to receive six months of guerrilla training at the Minas del Frio camp in Cuba's Sierra Maestra Mountains.

Using false identity papers, most of these men returned to the Dominican Republic, where they served as the hard core of a guerrilla operation which was launched on November 29, 1963. Over 120 guerrillas began operating in six areas: Altamira, Bonao, Enriquillo, San José de las Matas, San Francisco de Macorís, and Miches. The government —the Triumvirate—charged that the goal of the rebels was "to establish a Communist dictatorship."

Once again the Dominican armed forces moved effectively, and within a month the guerrilla bands had been wiped out. On the night of December 21 Army patrols located the last substantial group in the mountains west of San José de las Matas, and in the resulting action five guerrillas were captured and fifteen were killed. Among the dead was Manuel Tavárez Justo, head of the June 14th and "supreme commander" of the rebels. Altogether, the government reported, thirty-one guerrillas had been killed and ninety-two captured (most of whom were subsequently deported the following year).

Not only had Castro trained the guerrillas and sent them to launch the uprising, he also attempted to send them weapons. On December 6 a shipment of arms and ammunition was captured which had been sent from Cuba aboard a Cuban Navy vessel and transferred at sea to a Dominican fishing ship, the *Scarlet Woman*. Four men who had landed with the weapons were also captured.

When did the planning for the April 1965 uprising begin? Since Communists are always in a state of conspiracy, the moment when the plot was spawned cannot be pinpointed. In all likelihood, however, the conspiracy was given a considerable impetus at a secret meeting held in Havana of representatives of all Latin American Communist parties. At this conference, in November 1964, a decision was made to step up subversive efforts throughout the Hemisphere, and this included the Dominican Republic.

The Communists probably did not plan to launch their own rebellion openly. Undoubtedly aware of the pro-Bosch conspiracy, they would wait until this got started, and then move in—much as they moved into the Cuban government once Castro had already come to power. Highly significant is a "manifesto" issued on March 16, 1965—over a month before the civil war began—by the *Partido Socialista Popular*, another of the Dominican Republic's Communist parties. Ominously and prophetically, the statement declared:

"A growing popular clamor is rising throughout the country in favor of the return of Professor Juan Bosch. . . . This victory can only be achieved through the mobilization and the active struggle of all the patriotic sectors of our country. . . . Concrete actions by the masses . . . [are] imperative. . . . All the people, fight in the streets, in the plazas, in the factories, in the fields, for the return of

President Bosch at the front of the constitutional government!"

The return of Bosch, the Communists admitted, however, "does not signify the solution of the national problems." The return of Bosch through "popular action" would be "a step of extraordinary advance in the integration of the forces which will lead to the general emancipation of the Dominican people." Bosch's return, the Communists were saying, would be a step, but only a step, toward their eventual goal: "socialist democracy," i.e., Communism.

Within hours after the pro-Bosch military made their move in April, the Communist presence in the rebellion became apparent. The executions, the arming of civilians, the attacks on foreigners, the setting up of strongpoints, the leading of mobs to the offices of anti-Communist newspapers and political parties—all of these were traditional Communist tactics in a revolutionary situation. The rebels took over Radio Santo Domingo and it became an echo of Radio Habana Cuba: denouncing of the "oligarchies," calls to the "masses," violent attacks on the United States, abolishing the rank of general (à la Castro), declaration of "the dictatorship of the proletariat" and the "Free Territory of the Dominican Republic" (à la Cuba's claim to be the "Free Territory of the Americas").

There are three Communist parties in the Dominican Republic. The largest is the June 14th (APCJ), with a membership estimated at somewhere around 4000 militants. Its strength lies among students and workers, and Castro's influence is considerable. The *Partido Socialista Popular Dominicano* (PSPD), with approximately 1000 members, is Moscow-oriented. The *Movimiento Popular Dominicano* (MPD) has only about 500 members, but it closely follows the aggressive Communist Chinese line. (A fourth party that is occasionally mentioned, the *Partido Nacionalista Revolucionario,* is inactive and largely a paper organization.)

Despite any ideological differences they might have, the three Communist parties worked in unison when the rebellion broke out. The rapid and effective manner in which they began operating demonstrated the careful planning with which they had prepared themselves for revolution.

As soon as the military launched their uprising on April 24, the Communist leaders went into action. They armed themselves and their key followers, who were assigned to tasks in various parts of the city. Communists were ordered to incite civilian crowds that were gathering on the streets, and to organize rallies and demonstrations in favor of Bosch.

The following morning, armed PSPD members harangued crowds gathered in the downtown Parque Independencia. Among the speakers were Diomedes Mercedes Batista (who had traveled to Cuba in 1963), Narciso Isa Conde (a member of the PSPD Central Committee), and Asdrúbal Ulises Domíngues Guerrero (who had received training in Russia in 1962). Later, Communist mobile loudspeaker units drove through the city urging the citizenry to join the rebellion.

It was on this second day of the uprising that the Communists engineered an event that almost completely placed the revolt in their hands, at least for a while. Several thousand weapons, ranging from hand grenades to machine guns, were loaded on trucks at the 27th of February Army camp and driven to downtown Santo Domingo. There they were handed out to civilians. Top Communists helped Army rebels to distribute the weapons, and in some cases they actually controlled the distribution, thus seeing that their followers received arms. Among the Communists who took part in the handing out of weapons were: Fidelio Despradel Roque (a founder of the APCJ who had received guerrilla training in Cuba and was a leader of the abortive 1963 guerrilla operation); Félix Servio Ducoudray Mansfield, Jr. (a PSPD leader who had received indoctrination in Russia, worked in Cuba in 1960 for the New China News Agency, then visited Communist China, traveling on a Cuban passport); Juan Ducoudray Mansfield (Felix's brother, also a PSPD leader who had traveled to Russia, Communist China and Poland, and to Cuba, where he prepared scripts for broadcasts beamed toward the Dominican Republic); Hugo Tolentino Dipp (PSPD leader, guerrilla training in Cuba); Daniel Ozuna Hernandez (APCJ leader, survivor of the 1963 guerrilla operation); and Buenaventura Johnson Pimentel (member of the PSPD's Central Committee, possibly also a member of the APCJ).

To further prepare for street fighting, bottles (many removed from a Pepsi-Cola plant) were distributed to civilian rebels. These were filled with gasoline taken from tank trucks and filling stations, and they thus made "Molotov cocktails," particularly useful when fighting tanks.

The rebel radio station issued a call for a march on the National Palace, and several thousand civilians, armed with everything from clubs to rifles, responded and seized the building. Among the civilians was an armed Communist group, including PSPD members who had received guerrilla training in Cuba.

Leaders of Bosch's *Partido Revolucionario Dominicano* (PRD) arrived at the Palace and advocated setting up a temporary government under Rafael Molina Ureña until Bosch could be brought back. Other factions urged different steps, including the establishment of a military junta, but the PRD view prevailed, and Ureña took over as Provisional President. Communists actively participated in the heated discussions, siding with the Bosch people. Among the Communists present were Facundo Gomez (PSPD member who was part owner of the *Scarlet Woman,* the vessel which landed the Cuban weapons in December, 1963); Luis Gomez Perez (PSPD Central Committee, trained in Czechoslovakia); Antonio Emilio José Isa Conde (PSPD student agitator who received guerrilla training in Cuba and money in Prague) and his brother Narciso (PSPD Central Committee); Ema Tavarez Justo (APCJ student agitator and sister of APCJ

Leader Manuel Tavares Justo, killed in the 1963 guerrilla operation); and a number of other leading figures from the Communist parties, including Mercedes Batista, Ozuna Hernandez, and Lora Vicente (all previously identified). "President" Ureña appointed Alejandro Lajara Gonzalez (an APCJ member who earlier in the day had been busy distributing weapons to civilians) to the post of Deputy Director of Investigation.

Communist agitators incited the armed mobs to burn and destroy property. Civilians looted stores and homes, and Communists and hoodlums made a special point of killing policemen. The plant of the anti-Communist newspaper, *Prensa Libre*, was seized, and Communists immediately made preparations to print propaganda leaflets. The offices of three anti-Communist political parties, *Union Civica Nacional*, *Partido Liberal Revolucionista*, and *Vanguardia Revolucionaria Dominicana*, were sacked by mobs.

The Communists prepared themselves militarily. Additional weapons were obtained and distributed, para-military units were organized, strongpoints were established at strategic locations. Directing the Communist military activities was Manuel Gonzalez Gonzalez, a veteran of the Spanish Civil War who came to the Dominican Republic in 1940. A Communist, he joined the PSPD and rose to membership in the Central Committee. He was reported to be an agent of G-2, Castro's intelligence service. Assisting Gonzalez was Manuel Escobar Alfonseca, a prominent PSPD member who had received training behind the Iron Curtain in 1963.

Strongholds were established in a building on Arzobispo Portes Avenue (PSPD), on José Gabriel Garcia Street in the Ciudad Nueva low-cost housing area (APCJ), in a building at the corner of Arzobispo Merino and Luperon Streets (machine guns were set up on the roof), and at Arzobispo Portes and Sanchez Streets. Juan Miguel Roman Diaz (a member of the APCJ Central Committee and survivor of the 1963 guerrilla operation) commanded a combination prison, arsenal and strongpoint at the corner of Estrelleta and Arzobispo Nouel Streets. Gonzalez Gonzalez set up a "comando" in a building on the corner of El Conde and Hostos Streets. Another Communist group, calling itself the "Luperon Comando," was established at the corner of Hostos and Luperon Streets. Strongholds were established on Caracas Street, on Juan de Morpha Street and on Bolivar Avenue, as well as at other locations.

On April 26, General Wessin made his first move, sending his planes to bomb and strafe rebel positions. Public resentment was aroused, and the air attacks provided the Communists with a propaganda weapon. The rebel radio gave the names and addresses of Wessin's fliers and urged the public to sack these houses.

The distribution of weapons and the making of Molotov cocktails continued. Ema Tavarez Justo, Antonio Isa Conde, and other agitators continued haranguing crowds, and distributing mimeographed flysheets. These called for the formation of "common units of soldiers and civilians" and of "people's combat units" (*militia à la Castro*).

The effectiveness with which the Communist apparatus operated, combined with the arming of Communist-led civilians, caused a major shift within the top leadership of the rebel movement. Faced with mob violence which it could not control, frightened by the attacks of Wessin's warplanes, the PRD leadership dissolved. Molina Ureña gave up the "presidency," and several other PRD leaders, including José Pena Gomez, Maximo Lovaton Pittaluga, and Antonio Martínez Francisco, abandoned the rebel side. Martínez Francisco, secretary-general of the PRD, went to the loyalist Air Force base at San Isidro and appealed to the rebels to lay down their arms.

Approximately a thousand troops of the Regular Army had participated in the original revolt. As the Communists poured out weapons to civilians, these latter soon greatly outnumbered the soldiers. The rebel Army officers could not control the mobs; the Communists could. The fomenting and directing of mob violence is a tool with which the Communists have had considerable experience over the years in many lands.

Still in exile in Puerto Rico, Juan Bosch, symbolic leader of the rebellion, seemed little aware of what was happening in his country. Visited on May 2 by a special emissary of President Johnson's, John Bartlow Martin, Bosch spoke meaninglessly of "a meeting of the congress," "general amnesty for everybody," and the return of "Molina to the palace." Concluded Martin: Bosch "was still dreaming of the old days."

The Communists, by April 28, dominated the rebel movement, but they were unable to—and it probably was not yet their purpose to—restore order. Shooting was widespread, and armed mobs roamed the city, terrorizing it, sacking stores, firing on foreign embassies. The junta based at San Isidro notified the American ambassador that it could no longer provide protection for American citizens, and the wheels were quickly set in motion for the landing of U.S. Marines.

On April 29 an armed mob launched an attack on the last loyalist stronghold in downtown Santo Domingo, the police-held Ozama Fortress on the Ozama River. The attack was directed by MPD leaders who had been in Cuba but APCJ and PSPD members also participated. After heavy fighting, the fortress fell on April 30, and with it the Communists captured a large amount of weapons and ammunition.

On April 29 a mob looted a large church and, roaming through the Ciudad Nueva area, echoed slogans so familiar in Cuba: "Fatherland or death!" and "*Viva* Castro!"

But a new element was now entering the scene of the Dominican tragedy. To protect its citizens and those of other countries, and to block the Communist takeover, the United States began to pour troops into Santo Domingo. Some 3000 Marines and paratroopers were flown into the city and San Isidro on April 29 and 30, and more would arrive in the following days.

In order to discuss this new turn of events, leaders of the APCJ, PSPD and MPD met with Benjamin Ramos Alvarez on April 29. Ramos was a high-level APCJ member and head of that party's District Committee for Santo Domingo. Leading Communists, including Gonzalez Gonzalez and the Ducoudray brothers, also conferred with rebel Army officers.

Although the rebel radio instructed rebels not to fire on the American forces, attacks and sniping continued. The U.S. troops did not fire unless fired upon first, but once they had been shot at, they replied, and it was estimated that rebel casualties in these incidents were running at two to one for every American casualty. Two APCJ units were especially active, one of which was led by Central Committeeman Roman Diaz (who was killed in a firefight on May 19).

In Havana, Fidel Castro, addressing a May Day rally, admitted the Communist link with the Dominican rebellion. He said: "We do not know how many Communists there are in Santo Domingo. It is possible there are few Communists. But without a doubt of any kind, any Communist in a struggle like that one does not side with the imperialists, does not side with the gorillas [military]. He fights because that is his revolutionary duty—alongside the Constitution, alongside the party that defends the Constitution, although that party declares itself non-Communist, although that party swears that it has nothing to do with the Communists."

The rebel radio asked that U.S. troops not be fired on, but a shortwave transmitter gave contrary instructions, urging rebels to shoot at "Yankees" on sight. In the Parque Independencia, a violent anti-American speech was delivered before a crowd by Edmundo Garcia Castillo, a member of the PSPD.

During the first days of May rebel leaders held a series of conferences regarding their future moves. Considerable thought was given to improving the structure of their "government" so that it could make a greater claim to legitimacy. There was also discussion around this time as to the advisability of the top Communist leaders withdrawing from open participation in the rebel movement. Two reasons seemed to counsel this move: to prepare for the possibility that the Communist leaders might have to go underground and to lend credence to rebel disavowals of the Communist role in the rebellion.

Although the lesser Communists were to continue fighting, a number of top Communists went into hiding, and others attempted to go into the interior of the country. They were under instructions to organize local party members for eventual guerrilla action. False identity cards were prepared for these top leaders.

MPD leaders, as well as those of the APCJ and the PSPD, began to go underground. In addition, MPD members were urged to obtain as many weapons as they could, to be hidden for possible use in future guerrilla warfare.

Having been prevented from seizing control of the Dominican Republic, the Communists were now laying the groundwork for new subversive efforts.

On May 11, in a radio address, Colonel Caamaño, declared: "Despite the tremendous propaganda by U.S. publicity organs based on the erratic or ill-intentioned reports by Ambassador Bennett, our revolutionary government is eminently democratic. I do not have to tell the people this, because they know why they are fighting and what flag they are under. It is superfluous to insist further on this, but in this respect I can only say that there is no deafer person than the one who does not want to hear. That version [regarding the Communist role] is a specious fabrication . . ."

By Caamaño's side when he delivered the speech was Héctor Aristy, who held the post of minister of the presidency. Ordinarily, this would be an administrative position—sort of a general manager of the presidential office—but Aristy appeared to play a considerably more important role. Invariably when Caamaño talked with foreign diplomats or correspondents, Aristy would be with him, ostensibly as a translator (although Caamaño speaks English well), but actually to counsel him and sometimes even to speak for him.

Before the rebellion, Aristy had been a playboy, a minor politician and a sometime conspirator. Once the rebellion started, the smoothness with which Aristy handled matters around Caamaño was noted, and there was some suspicion that he was a trained Communist agent, but most qualified observers labeled him simply as an "opportunist."

John Bartlow Martin, the U.S. presidential emissary, conferred with Caamaño and noticed the ubiquitous presence of Aristy. On one occasion Martin and the nuncio were trying to convince Caamaño to confer with General Imbert, but Caamaño insisted that before he would do this, Imbert had to get rid of General Wessin and two other officers. Writing in *Life* magazine, Martin recalled:

> The nuncio said, ". . . We must talk about peace. Will you talk at the *nunciatura?*"
>
> Caamaño said, "No, I cannot go there."
>
> I said, "Well, where can you go? Let's find a place," and touched his sleeve and said, "Let's look at the map."
>
> I wanted to get him alone—for the first time. I took him to the far end of the table and asked in a low voice, "Are you a free agent?"
>
> He said, "I am a free agent."
>
> "Can you leave here?"
>
> He hesitated, said, "My people say that talking won't do any good as long as those three are there. If I did, I'd be out."
>
> "That's what I'm asking you—are you a free agent? Who would put you 'out'? Who are 'your people'?"
>
> "My *militantes.* The cabinet. Some senators."
>
> *Militantes,* in this cloudy context, could mean either soldiers, like himself, who had defected, or Castro-Communists. I asked, "Who are the *militantes?*"
>
> Caamaño hesitated again, then said, "The officers."
>
> I said, "Not the Communists?"

52

He said, "There are no Communists."

I said, "We know there are. What I am asking is whether you are free of them."

He said, looking away, speaking hesitantly, "There may be individual Communists in my area. But they are not in the leadership. After we get this over, we get rid of them."

I was far from sure. And I think he was, too.

This was not the only time that Caamaño admitted to the Communist presence in the revolution. The Organization of American States sent a special committee to Santo Domingo (see Chapter VI), and when it later returned to Washington, Mexico's O.A.S. ambassador raised the question of Communist infiltration in the rebel movement.

To this, the chairman of the committee, Argentina's O.A.S. ambassador, Ricardo M. Colombo, replied: ". . . We spoke with the different men who were in this rebel grouping and, a notable thing, from the head of the revolution, Colonel Caamaño, to someone known as minister of the presidency, they recognized that they [the Communists] were their great problem. They explained to a certain extent briefly the process of the history of the Dominican Republic, they confessed to us how gradually a number of elements were being incorporated with them whom they called Communists, and that their problem was to avoid infiltration for the purpose of springing a surprise and seizing control. They said this clearly, and even at one point . . . I spoke with Colonel Caamaño and asked him in a friendly way whether he honestly believed that such infiltration existed. He confirmed this to me, but he gave me the impression that he had the courage to face it."

The Communists had again failed in their effort to conquer the Dominican Republic. But Ernesto Guevara, the master planner and wily executor of Cuban subversion, once wrote: "The result of the struggles of today does not matter. That one or another movement be put down transitorily is not important for the final result. Decisive is the resolution for struggle which ripens day by day . . ."

In the Dominican Republic, the Communists were already preparing for a new effort, a new struggle, a new battle.

CHAPTER V
The U.S. Role

A FEW DAYS after the Bay of Pigs disaster, the late President John F. Kennedy declared: "Any unilateral American intervention, in the absence of an external attack upon ourselves or an ally, would have been contrary to our traditions and to our international obligations. But let the record show that our restraint is not inexhaustible. Should it ever appear that the inter-American doctrine of nonintervention merely conceals or excuses a policy of non-action—if the nations of this Hemisphere should fail to meet their commitments against outside Communist penetration—then I want it clearly understood that this government will not hesitate in meeting its primary obligations, which are to the security of our nation. Should that time ever come, we do not intend to be lectured on 'intervention' by those whose character was stamped for all time on the bloody streets of Budapest."

Just four years later, these words of President Kennedy's were to become a cornerstone of the U.S. move into the Dominican Republic.

The primary obligations of the U.S. government include the protection of its citizens—which is the obligation of any government—and it fell upon President Kennedy's successor to decide whether to send troops to protect the endangered Americans in the Dominican Republic. It was a decision that had to be made quickly. Secretary of State Dean Rusk later recalled how swiftly the situation changed: "Time factors were crucial. Earlier in the afternoon of April 28 the American ambassador reported that he was not prepared to recommend the use of American armed forces. At 5:15 he informed us that the situation had deteriorated very badly and very rapidly, that the police and military authorities had informed him that they could no longer control the situation: that American and foreign nationals were in desperate danger and that outside forces were required . . . [The O.A.S. did] not have standby forces or the political machinery for the immediate decisions required to deal with such urgent contingencies."

President Johnson himself, in a television address on May 2, described the developments leading to his decision to land American forces:

". . . From Saturday to Wednesday, the danger was mounting. Even though we were deeply saddened by bloodshed and violence in a close and friendly neighbor, we had no desire to interfere in the affairs of a sister republic.

"On Wednesday afternoon there was no longer any choice for the man who is your President. I was sitting in my little office reviewing the world situation with Secretary Rusk, Secretary McNamara and Mr. McGeorge Bundy. Shortly after three o'clock, I received a cable from our ambassador, and he said that things were in danger; he had been informed the chief of police and governmental authorities could no longer protect us. We immediately started the necessary conference calls to be prepared.

"At 5:14, almost two hours later, we received a cable that was labeled 'critic,' a word that is reserved for only the most urgent and immediate matters of national security.

"The cable reported that Dominican law enforcement and military officials had informed our embassy that the situation was completely out of control and that the police and the government could no longer give any guarantee concerning the safety of Americans or any foreign nationals.

"Ambassador Bennett, who is one of our most experienced Foreign Service officers, went on in that cable to say that only an immediate landing of American forces could safeguard and protect the lives of thousands of Americans and thousands of other citizens of some thirty other countries. Ambassador Bennett urged your President to order an immediate landing.

"In this situation, hesitation and vacillation could mean death for many of our people, as well as many of the citizens of other lands.

"I thought that we could not, and we did not, hesitate. Our forces, American forces, were ordered in immediately to protect American lives."

For decades the United States had followed a policy of not intervening militarily in Latin American countries, and now the seeming abandonment* of this policy was coming under some criticism. To this, President Johnson replied: "There may be those in our own country who say that such action was good, but we should have waited, or we should have delayed, or we should have consulted further, or we should have called a meeting. But from the very beginning, the United States, at my instructions, had worked for a ceasefire beginning the Saturday the revolution took place. The matter was before the O.A.S. Peace Committee on Tuesday, at our suggestion. It was before the full Council on Wednesday . . .

"When that cable arrived, when our entire country team in the Dominican Republic, made up of nine men—one from the army, navy and air force, our ambassador, our A.I.D. man, and others—said to your President unanimously: Mr. President, if you do not send forces immediately, men and women—Americans and those of other lands—will die in the streets—well, I knew there was no time to talk, to consult or to delay."

The United States did not view its move into the Dominican Republic in the classic terms of intervention to exact tribute, protect holdings or impose a government. In an interview with the Associated

---

* Actually, during the 1956–1958 Cuban civil war, American forces twice went on Cuban soil: once to protect the pumping station which supplied water for the Guantanamo naval base, and once to cover the evacuation of American civilians from an isolated area of war-torn Oriente Province.

Press, Secretary Rusk stated: "Our decision to send troops to the Dominican Republic was aimed at saving lives. The situation in the Dominican Republic was one of anarchy. . . . Under similar circumstances governments from time immemorial have been recognized to have not merely the right but the obligation to take whatever action is necessary to save the lives of their nationals. It had nothing to do with nineteenth century types of intervention. . . . There is voluminous evidence to indicate that the Marines arrived just in time to avoid a major calamity."

The United States trod a careful road in the Dominican Republic. Although it had landed troops, it made it clear that—except for preventing a Communist takeover—it was neutral and not taking sides in the Dominican conflict. It could have pursued a different policy which might have averted much of the criticism of "intervention," but a policy which would have required the United States to align itself with one of the factions. Thomas C. Mann, Under Secretary of State for Economic Affairs and a key adviser to President Johnson on Latin American affairs, explained in an interview in *The New York Times:*

"Had the United States been interested in merely the form of legalistic procedures rather than the substance of the fundamental rights of a nation under the O.A.S. Charter, it could have recognized the only organized group existing at that time and claiming to be the government [the military junta].

"It could then have responded to a request from

the newly recognized group to send in armed forces. The United States did not follow such a course of action, because this would have amounted to taking sides in the internal struggle. Clearly such a course of action would have been inconsistent with the principles that govern the inter-American system."

The protection and evacuation of civilians was the immediate aim of the American forces that landed. Amidst the rapidly deteriorating situation, however, another dangerous problem emerged with ominous swiftness. This problem was the one to which President Kennedy had directly referred in his April 20, 1961, speech: the threat of a Communist takeover. Well-trained, well-disciplined, well-armed, the small but tight and effective Communist group had been preparing for revolution for a long time, and now it was moving to take advantage of the chaotic state of affairs in order to win control of the revolutionary movement. As early as April 30, President Johnson in a radio-television address, warned:

". . . There are signs that people trained outside the Dominican Republic are seeking to gain control. Thus the legitimate aspirations of the Dominican people and most of their leaders for progress, democracy and social justice are threatened and so are the principles of the inter-American system.

"The inter-American system, and its principal organ, the Organization of American States, have a grave and immediate responsibility. It is important that prompt action be taken."

And in his May 2 speech President Johnson declared: "The revolutionary movement took a tragic turn. Communist leaders, many of them trained in Cuba, seeing a chance to increase disorder, to gain a foothold, joined the revolution. They took increasing control. And what began as a popular democratic revolution, committed to democracy and social justice, very shortly moved and was taken over and really seized and placed into the hands of a band of Communist conspirators.

"Many of the original leaders of the rebellion, the followers of President Bosch, took refuge in foreign embassies because they had been superseded by other evil forces. . . .

"The American nations cannot, must not and will not permit the establishment of another Communist government in the Western Hemisphere. This was the unanimous view of all the American nations when, in January, 1962, they declared, and I quote: 'The principles of Communism are incompatible with the principles of the inter-American system.'

"This is what our beloved President John F. Kennedy meant when, less than a week before his death, he told us: 'We in this Hemisphere must also use every resource at our command to prevent the establishment of another Cuba in this Hemisphere. . . .'

"This is and this will be the common action and the common purpose of the democratic forces of the Hemisphere. For the danger is also a common danger, and the principles are common principles."

At what point did the Communist threat become

a major source of concern? Under Secretary Mann answered the question thus in his aforementioned interview: "Our intelligence from the very beginning was that the revolutionary movement itself was probably led by elements in the Dominican Revolutionary (pro-Bosch) Party, but it was clear very early that elements of the three Communist parties in the Dominican Republic succeeded in organizing, arming and moving into the streets very sizable para-military forces. This was known from the beginning . . . of the revolt."

Secretary Rusk stated: "Had they [the Communists] succeeded in establishing a government, the Communist seizure of power would in all likelihood have been irreversible, thus frustrating the declared principles of the O.A.S. We acted to preserve the freedom of choice of the Dominican people until the O.A.S. could take charge and insure that its principles were carried out. It is now doing so."

The United States, having acted by itself under the stress of the emergency, did not attempt to continue a unilateral policy, but rather sought the counsel and assistance of other parties and nations. President Johnson conferred with leading figures of Latin America's "liberal left," ex-Presidents Rómulo Betancourt of Venezuela and José Figueres of Costa Rica, and Luis Muñoz Marín, former governor and now a senator of Puerto Rico. The United States encouraged and led the O.A.S. into taking an increasingly important role in the Dominican crisis. In Santo Domingo, U.S. officials worked closely with the Papal Nuncio and O.A.S. representatives seeking an effective ceasefire.

The United States kept the United Nations informed of developments in the Dominican Republic. U.S. Delegate Adlai Stevenson, while holding to the traditional American viewpoint that Hemisphere problems should be left to the O.A.S., nevertheless voted for a Security Council resolution which called for "a strict ceasefire" and requested UN Secretary-General U Thant to send "a representative to the Dominican Republic for the purpose of reporting to the Security Council on the present situation."

Hardly had the Dominican rebellion flared when President Johnson summoned John Bartlow Martin to Washington for conferences. Martin had been U.S. ambassador to the Dominican Republic during Bosch's presidency, and he had been on good terms with Bosch. Later, as Martin wrote in an article in *Life* magazine, "The President asked me to go to Santo Domingo to do everything possible to assist William Tapley Bennett, Jr., our ambassador there, to open up contact with the rebels and keep the President closely informed of the situation, and to help the Organization of American States and our people stop the bloodshed and restore peace."

Martin flew to Santo Domingo and immediately plunged into a tireless series of conferences. Martin had come, he wrote, "with grave misgivings . . . People were saying that the revolt was Communist-led. Was it really?" Martin soon found his answer:

"At the outset, the revolt had been a well-planned and well-executed movement led principally by Juan Bosch's P.R.D. . . . especially by young men passionately dedicated to Bosch's—and our—ideals of liberty and justice.

"Almost immediately the revolt had been joined by elements of the military. Some were simply adventurers. But others were crack troops . . . sickened by the corruption of the generals in the Reid regime. . . .

"And almost immediately the revolt had been joined, too, by dedicated Communists. . . .

"And, finally, the rebellion had been joined by hundreds, perhaps thousands, of ordinary Dominicans who had emerged from Trujillo's tyranny and who had been told by me and others that the U.S. would help them get a better life. They had voted for Bosch, and they had seen the cost of living rising and their hopes disappearing during the Reid regime.

"That, then, was how the revolt had begun. But in a flash, almost as rapid and blinding as nuclear fusion, it had changed. The military men who sided with the civilian rebels had looted the arsenals of huge quantities of weapons. Quickly they handed out guns on street corners to anybody. Quickly they forced filling station operators to fill bottles brought by anybody. From these they made Molotov cocktails.

"The slaughter began. . . .

"The bloodbath drowned the ideals and purposes which had created the rebellion . . . Each man had rebelled for his own reasons—Boschist idealism, revenge, plunder, Communist directive. Now, all had become extremists in the true sense of the word —men of violence, almost animals. . . .

"To people like this, all doors are shut—except the Communist doors."

A primary goal sought by Martin and other American officials was some sort of political solution which would end the fighting and start the Dominican people back on the road to democratic self-rule. The junta at San Isidro was too reminiscent of traditional military dictatorships. Its replacement would be an encouraging step forward. In the course of his many conferences, Martin had talked with General Imbert, whose home within the International Safety Zone was guarded by his personal troops. Now, late on the night of May 3, Martin recalled:

> Antonio Imbert called and asked me to come to his house again. He said that various people, both military and civilians, had told him they could support neither the rebels nor the San Isidro crowd. They had told him that those old generals must leave the country, that Colonel Benoit's three-man military junta must be reconstituted, that only Imbert was strong enough to do it.
>
> I asked, "Do you want to do it?"
>
> He said, "I do it. For my country. Not for myself. Whatta hell I want to get into this mess for? I can sit here quiet."
>
> I said, "We are not going to support any military dictatorship."
>
> "I know."

"And I don't think any better of the old generals than you do. Can you get rid of them?"

"I fix." [Subsequently Imbert retired and deported six generals.]

"What about the junta?"

"We leave one of them in, Colonel Benoit. The others resign."

"Will they?"

"Su-u-ure," drawing it out, a way he has.

"What kind of a government is this going to be? Who'll be in it?"

"No politicians, you can be sure of that, Mr. Martin."

He began naming names. To himself and Colonel Benoit, he would add three civilians. He wanted the civilians to be nonpolitical—"politicians have ruined my country." He wanted men of stature, not identified with either side in the present conflict.

On May 7 a five-man group, headed by Imbert, was sworn in as a "Government of National Reconstruction." The ceremony was conducted in the Senate chamber in an area held by loyalist forces near the Embajador Hotel (but outside the International Zone), and afterwards Imbert delivered a speech in which he said the new government would work for peace and democracy.

The United States, still neutral, still seeking a solution, tried to get Imbert and Caamaño together for talks. Caamaño was reluctant, but on May 11 he agreed to consult his advisers about such a meeting and said he would notify the nuncio at three that afternoon. Martin described what followed:

"Back at the chancellery we waited. Two hours

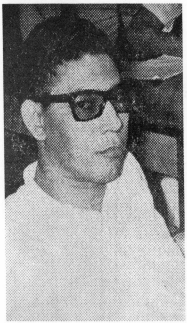

[6] Two of the Communist and Castroist leaders identified as operating among the rebel forces are: *top foreground,* Juan Ducoudray Mansfield, described as a long time leader of the Dominican Communist Party (shown here in 1961 with Aleksei Kosygin, *background,* now Premier of the Soviet Union); and *bottom,* Daniel Ozuna Hernandez, one of the leaders of the 14th of June movement.

[7] *top,* Members of the Brazilian Escuela Infantry Regiment are part of the Inter-American Force in the Dominican Republic.

[8] *bottom,* The first troops of the Inter-American Force to reach the Dominican Republic were a 250-man contingent of Honduran soldiers, including infantrymen, medical corpsmen, military police, and others.

[9] Members of the Costa Rican military contingent for the Inter-American Peace Force arrive by plane at Santo Domingo on May 15.

[10] *top,* Members of the OEA stand at attention in Santo Domingo during a ceremony before the unit's first patrol.

[11] *bottom,* A U.S. Military Police captain briefs a patrol of Honduran and U.S. Military Police on the routes they will cover. The letters OEA (for Organizacion de Los Estados Americanos) are on the helmets and arm bands of the newly formed force.

passed. Three. Just past 3 P.M., the nuncio called; [Martin and an aide] hurried to him.

"Caamaño had called the nuncio 20 minutes earlier and said that the meeting was off. According to Caamaño 'troops of Wessin' [who controlled no troops in the capital] had attacked the Dragon Restaurant inside the rebel area, using U.S. forces as cover, and had killed one rebel and wounded others.

"We hurried off to find out what had happened at the restaurant. But then Caamaño's right-hand military man called and told us that American troops across the river were killing every unarmed civilian who showed himself. Tonight, he threatened, the rebels would 'level' the flour mill on the American-held side of the river.

"Suspicion grew that the rebels did not want to talk, that they were creating incidents in order to sabotage the talks—not Caamaño himself, but the Communists behind him."

The O.A.S. team, also trying to bring Imbert and Caamaño together at the conference table, encountered the same difficulties as Martin (see Chapter VI). To a reporter, Martin commented: "Believe me, that violence was prepared by the Communists who were making sure that we wouldn't come to an agreement with Caamaño Deñó. The Communists didn't want a peaceful solution like that. They wanted us booby-trapped into a Budapest in the Dominican Republic. This was a sophisticated thing, like the Communists in Spain who killed anybody who tried to make a compromise."

On May 16 a high-level U.S. mission flew to Santo Domingo. It was headed by McGeorge Bundy, presidential assistant for national security affairs, and it included Under Secretary of Defense Cyrus R. Vance, Under Secretary Thomas Mann, and Jack Hood Vaughn, Assistant Secretary of State for Inter-American Affairs. The group carried with them a list of ten or so names of Dominican figures who might be acceptable to both the Imbert group as well as the non-Communist elements on the rebel side. Among those whose names were on the list was Antonio Guzmán Silvestro, a wealthy landowner who had served as minister of agriculture during Bosch's presidency.

At the O.A.S., American Ambassador Ellsworth Bunker gave a report on the work of the U.S. mission in Santo Domingo. Ambassador Bunker said: "Their instructions were to lend maximum assistance to the O.A.S. and to the people and the leaders of the Dominican Republic:

"To help bring an end to the fighting and bloodshed;

"To aid in the establishment of a broadly representative government based on democratic constitutional principles;

"To help eliminate the threat of present or future subversion of the government of the Dominican government by Communists or other extremist elements;

"To facilitate the arrangement for the inclusion of U.S. forces in the Inter-American Force and to plan the progressive reduction and eventual withdrawal of those forces as the O.A.S. succeeds in restoring peace and civil order."

Ambassador Bunker reported that, "despite the bitterness of the fighting and the intensive propaganda from both sides," the U.S. mission had found Dominican sentiment which favored "certain principles . . . essential to the establishment of a stable government." These principles were:

"First, civilian and military leaders on both sides recognize that the Communists present a continuing threat to any democratic government. They recognize that these Communists, some of them trained abroad, must be dealt with effectively, vigorously and definitively to prevent the Dominican government and people from falling under their control.

"Second, responsible Dominican leaders have discussed the making of a broadly based government of integrity and competence, vigorously excluding the extreme right and extreme left. There is reason to believe that able and experienced men of this type, reflecting a wide spectrum of political, economic and social views, are available to serve in a new government.

"Third, the government must be essentially civilian, and if possible, the new chiefs of the military services should be accessible to both factions so as to avoid friction and to facilitate separation of the armed forces from politics."

A new problem arose in the efforts to set up a compromise government. General Imbert, having taken over as the head of the loyalist regime, began to get it to function like a government once more. In addition, his troops launched an offensive May 15 against a rebel-held area in a section of the city north of the U.S.-controlled corridor. In a week of fierce fighting, the Imbert troops were able to overrun the rebel stronghold. This left the rebels in control of only a small downtown area, completely surrounded by American land and sea forces. The victory greatly enhanced Imbert's position, and he began to receive messages of support from throughout the country, including a good many from people who had previously been "fence-sitting."

The United States and the Organization of American States continued their efforts to resolve the bitter and extremely difficult Dominican problem. One accomplishment was the achieving of a more effective ceasefire than the previous ones.

The American goal for the Dominican people remained as it had been stated by President Johnson on May 2:

"The form and the nature of the free Dominican government, I assure you, is solely a matter for the Dominican people, but we do know what kind of government we hope to see in the Dominican Republic. For that is carefully spelled out in the treaties and the agreements which make up the fabric of the inter-American system. It is expressed, time and time again, in the words of our statesmen and the values and hopes which bind us all together.

"We hope to see a government freely chosen by the will of all the people.

"We hope to see a government dedicated to social justice for every citizen.

"We hope to see a government working, every hour of every day, to feeding the hungry, to educating the ignorant, to healing the sick—a government whose only concern is the progress and the elevation and the welfare of all the people."

CHAPTER VI
The O.A.S.

THE DOMINICAN PEOPLE had to make a crucial decision—whether to support the rebellion.

The United States had to make a crucial decision—whether to land troops.

But perhaps the most significant decision of all had to be made by the Organization of American States. In the face of the Dominican crisis, would it act effectively, or would it fail to do anything, and thus confirm what its critics have said, that it was only a paper organization?

The Dominican people would live on. The United States would continue to be. The decisions to be made by the O.A.S., however, might well determine whether it was to fade away—or to emerge as a stronger and more influential organization than ever before.

The Dominican problem first officially came to the attention of the O.A.S. on Tuesday, April 27. At noon on that day, the United States called for a meeting of the Inter-American Peace Committee. The committee met at four that afternoon and heard a report by Dominican Ambassador José Antonio Bonilla Atiles on events in his country. The committee considered whether it had jurisdiction in the Dominican case, but it took no decision other than to keep informed of developments.

The following morning, the regular meeting of the O.A.S. Council was held, and Ambassador Bonilla again gave a report, emphasizing Castro-Communist participation in the rebellion.

That evening, all the chiefs of Latin American diplomatic missions in Washington were informed, in person and by telephone, of the decision by the United States to land troops in the Dominican Republic. The United States requested a special meeting of the O.A.S. Council for the following morning.

The Council convened at 10:30 the next morning in a secret session, and American Ambassador Ellsworth Bunker explained why the United States had had to land troops: "During the afternoon of yesterday it became apparent that a complete breakdown of public order had taken place in the Dominican Republic. . . . Armed civilians were reported to be roaming through the streets, shooting indiscriminately and looting stores. The embassy reported that the leadership of the rebellious forces had very clearly fallen into hands of extreme left-wing Castro-Communist leaders, with some few army officers who were cooperating. Responsible supporters of Mr. Bosch and the leaders of his political party had abandoned the struggle . . ."

The Dominican ambassador again reported on the situation in his homeland, describing scenes of chaos, terror and Communist militancy. His own nephew, Rafael Bonilla Aybar, a well-known anti-Communist newspaperman, had narrowly escaped death by fleeing into the Guatemalan Embassy. (It was in search of Bonilla that the rebels had entered the Hotel Embajador and terrorized the Americans there.) Declared the Dominican ambassador: "Are they rebels? Do they fight for constitutionality? No, my dear friends: They are Communists."

The Council voted to send a telegram to Papal Nuncio Emanuelle Clarizio, dean of the diplomatic corps in Santo Domingo. The message requested the nuncio to convey to all Dominican factions the Council's hope for a cessation of "all armed actions and hostilities."

This call for a ceasefire was incorporated into a resolution formally adopted the following day by a vote of 16 to 0, with four abstentions (Chile, Mexico, Uruguay, and Venezuela). The ambassadors agreed:

1. To reiterate the call of April 29, 1965 upon all the authorities, the political groupings, and the opposing forces to pursue immediately all possible means by which a ceasefire may be established and all hostilities and military operations suspended in order to prevent any further tragic loss of life or injury as well as material damages in the sister Dominican Republic.

2. To make an urgent appeal to the same authorities, political groupings, and forces on both sides to permit the immediate establishment of an international zone of refuge, encompassing the geographic area of the city of Santo Domingo immediately surrounding the embassies of foreign gov-

ernments, the inviolability of which will be
respected by all opposing forces and within which
nationals of all countries will be given safe haven.

3. To inform the Security Council of the United
Nations of the text of this resolution pursuant to
Article 54 of the United Nations Charter.

It was Article 2 of this resolution which served as
the legal basis for the establishment of the "international safety zone" by the American forces. The resolution was adopted after the O.A.S. heard Ambassador Bunker declare:

". . . The government of the United States has
consistently urged on all the parties the necessity of
a ceasefire. Several ceasefires have actually been ar-
ranged, but none of them have been kept. And
since the Americans and other foreigners have been
in great danger, we have—at the same time that we
have been requesting a ceasefire on both sides—we
have evacuated some 1400 citizens of my country
and of other nations.

"Unfortunately, before the evacuation was completed, there was further deterioration rather than a
ceasefire, and an equal number of American citizens
and many more nationals of other countries are still
in the Dominican Republic. . . .

"Beginning today the United States Embassy has
been under heavy fire throughout the day, and according to our information the diplomatic inviolability of at least five American embassies has been
violated; one of them . . . the embassy of El Salvador, has been sacked and burned . . .

"We are . . . faced with an immediate problem of

76

how to restore law and order in order to protect not only the citizens of foreign countries, private and official; not only to proceed with evacuation in an orderly way; but also to stop the excessive vandalism which many people are wreaking on their fellow Dominican citizens. . . .

"The United States must therefore reserve its right to take the necessary measures to protect its own citizens and officials from violence in a situation of anarchy.

"There are many precedents for this kind of a situation. None of this is inconsistent with the inter-American obligations. We wholeheartedly subscribe to these obligatons, including the doctrine of nonintervention and self-determination.

"We are not talking about intruding in the domestic affairs of other countries; we are talking simply about the elementary duty to save lives in a situation where there is no authority able to accept responsibility for primary law and order. We believe that this is a matter of the greatest urgency for the O.A.S. to deal with within the family of the Hemisphere in which all of us have a great stake."

Ambassador Bunker continued with a warning and an offer: "I must state quite frankly to this Council that events are moving with great rapidity and it may not be easy for the Organization of American States to keep pace with those events, but I can assure you that the United States is prepared to transfer its responsibilities to the Organization of American States at the earliest possible moment."

Acting upon the request of the Chilean ambassador, the O.A.S. Council voted to convoke "a meeting of consultation of ministers of foreign affairs of the American republic." The agenda would be the "serious situation created by the armed strife in the Dominican Republic." Largely this would be a procedural matter, with the same ambassadors serving as delegates, but the change would emphasize the importance of the situation. The meeting would convene May 1 at the Pan American Union Building in Washington.

In a later session on April 30, Ambassador Bunker again reported on events in the Dominican Republic and stated, "I want to say again what I said yesterday, that is, that obviously it is the hope and wish of my country to remove our forces as rapidly as may be, and that we would certainly welcome the establishment of a multilateral force to safeguard the zone of refuge while this problem of evacuation continues." In addition, Bunker asserted, "It is extremely important that an O.A.S. official arrive in Santo Domingo as rapidly as possible." Acting as president of the O.A.S. Council, Bunker requested Secretary-General José A. Mora to fly to the troubled country, and Mora agreed to do so. From then on, Mora was to play an important role in the peace-seeking efforts in the Dominican Republic.

The doctrine of non-intervention is viewed as sacred by Latin Americans, and inevitably the United States came under criticism for landing troops in the Dominican Republic. Few Latin American officials or newspapers were willing to acknowledge publicly the urgent reasons that had compelled the United States to make its move—even though a good many Latin American citizens were among those saved by this military move.

When the meeting of consultation convened, the United States was assailed by a number of delegates. (Many were speaking for the record—privately they had expressed a realistic understanding of the need for rapid U.S. action in Santo Domingo.) The Venezuelan delegate, Enrique Tejera París, declared, "The landing in the territory of that sister republic of armed forces of the United States of America has been the cause of profound consternation in our countries." The Chilean delegate, Alejandro Magnet, read a statement issued by his country's minister of foreign relations, declaring: "With firmness we request from the O.A.S. the rejection of the unilateral intervention. . . . The government of Chile considers the presence of North American military forces in the Dominican Republic, even though to protect their co-nationals, as contrary to the Charter of the O.A.S. and to clear principles of international law, and requests their withdrawal . . ."

Ambassador Bunker replied to the criticism: ". . . This is not intervention in any sense by the United States in the affairs of the Dominican Republic. United States forces were dispatched purely and solely for humanitarian purposes for the protection of the lives not only of United States citizens, but the lives of citizens of other countries as well. . . . We are not talking about intruding in the domestic affairs of other countries. We are talking simply about the elementary duty to save lives in a situation where there is no authority able to accept responsibility for primary law and order. . . .

"Obviously we have no candidate for government in the Dominican Republic. This is a matter for the Dominican people themselves, and it is for us to find the means to assist the Dominican people to constitute a government which reflects their wishes and a government which can undertake the international obligations of the Hemisphere.

"I may add, Mr. Chairman, that the forces of the United States arrived barely in time to avoid far greater casualties and greater bloodshed than actually took place. At the time of the arrival of those forces, firing had begun on foreign nationals assembled at the polo grounds for the purpose of seeking evacuation from the republic . . ."

(Earlier, Bunker had pointed out that the United States had received "a number" of urgent requests from Latin American diplomats in Santo Domingo for American protection for their embassies.)

The O.A.S. got down to cases, and on May 1 it voted (19 in favor, Chile abstaining) to establish a committee composed of the delegates of Argentina, Brazil, Colombia, Guatemala and Panama. The committee was instructed:

> . . . To go immediately to the city of Santo Domingo, to do everything possible to obtain the reestablishment of peace and normal conditions, and to give priority to the following two functions:
> a. To offer its good offices to the Dominican

armed groups and political groups and to diplomatic representatives for the purpose of obtaining urgently:

i. a ceasefire; and

ii. the orderly evacuation of the persons who have taken asylum in the embassies and of all foreign citizens who desire to leave the Dominican Republic; and

b. To carry out an investigation of all aspects of the situation in the Dominican Republic that led to the convocation of this meeting . . .

The committee was also instructed to submit a report on the progress of its work "in the shortest time possible."

The committee was flown to San Isidro in an American plane. So confused were affairs in the Dominican Republic, that there were neither American nor Dominican officials on hand to greet the group. The 82nd Airborne, however, had set up headquarters in a hangar, and the O.A.S. officials took shelter there until they could be taken by helicopter into Santo Domingo.

The committee plunged into a series of conferences with the Papal Nuncio, American officials and the leaders of the two warring Dominican factions. The first message the committee sent back to the O.A.S. was, however, a humanitarian appeal for "foodstuffs, medicine and medical personnel." The message said, "The committee is convinced that this is the most urgent of the serious problems being faced, in order to prevent the possibility of epidemics and other calamities that could make the situation of the Dominican people even more difficult."

Latin American nations responded to the call. Panama sent nurses, Venezuela and Argentina sent doctors, and food and medical supplies came from Colombia, Brazil, Chile, Guatemala, Mexico, and Uruguay. Food shipments were also sent from the United States.

The committee had been specifically instructed to work for a ceasefire, and after several days of conferences, it got the leaders of the warring factions to sign (May 5) the "Act of Santo Domingo." Both sides agreed to:

. . . Ratify the ceasefire agreement signed on April 30 last.

. . . Accept the establishment of a safety zone in the city of Santo Domingo . . . [This was the first time the rebels formally accepted the existence of the zone.]

. . . Respect this safety zone . . .

. . . Undertake to give all necessary facilities to the International Red Cross or to the international agency that the Organization of American States may designate to carry out in any part of the city of Santo Domingo or of the Dominican Republic the distribution of food, medicine and medical and hospital equipment . . .

. . . Provide all necessary safety measures for the evacuation of asylees in foreign embassies . . .

. . . Respect the diplomatic missions . . .

. . . Accept and recognize the full competence of the special committee appointed by the Tenth Meeting of Consultation of Ministers of Foreign Affairs, for purposes of the faithful observance of what is agreed to in this agreement.

The ceasefire would be little heeded by either

side, but even so, the O.A.S. was now beginning to assert its authority. And the Dominicans were recognizing and accepting this authority.

At the O.A.S. in Washington, the United States was seeking to have that body take an even more important step, a truly historic step. On May 3 the United States presented a draft resolution requesting the "governments of American states that are capable of doing so to make contingents of their military, naval, air, and police forces available to the meeting of consultation in order to assist in carrying out the mission of the committee." Under the diplomatic phraseology, the United States was calling for the establishment of the first inter-American military force. Ambassador Bunker assured the delegates that "the forces of the United States which are already there, or to be sent there, would be included, naturally, with all other forces."

Several of the delegates opposed the creation of an inter-American force. There was still concern over the landing of U.S. troops. On May 3, however, the Costa Rican delegate, Gonzalo J. Facio, delivered a blunt speech:

"Until now we have heard talk with impressionable insistence of a single principle of the inter-American system: the principle of non-intervention. It would appear as if this were the only principle that governs inter-American relations. The Costa Rican delegation does not share that criterion. It believes the system is ruled by a series of principles of great importance, without it being possible to subordinate their validity to the principle of non-intervention. There is, for example, the principle of respect for human rights, the principle of the effective exercise of representative democracy as a *sine qua non* condition of continental solidarity, there is the principle of the peaceful settlement of controversies, and furthermore there is the fundamental proposition of the Charter of offering the American man a land of liberty and an atmosphere favorable for the development of his personality and the realization of his just aspirations.

"All those principles, and much more, are at stake in the tragic situation which the Dominican Republic today lives—not only that of non-intervention. For my delegation it is inconceivable that the meeting of foreign ministers shuts its eyes to the sad events in Quisqueya [Dominican Republic] and occupies itself solely with determining whether or not the principle of non-intervention has been violated. . . .

"It may be that the government of the United States, in its anxiety to avert worse evils, has violated the principle of non-intervention. But that should not prevent us from acting to repair the wrong and to helping our brothers. Other countries continually violate other principles of the Charter, and although this is very lamentable, the work of the O.A.S. is not paralyzed in order to dedicate itself to lamenting those violations.

"It is true that we cannot accept as good that the United States decides for itself when it should send troops to prevent the triumph or the defeat of a rebellion. But neither can we accept as good that anarchy reigns in a brother country, and that there can be established in it, as a result, a tyrannical regime which, like that of Cuba, would be a constant fountain of inter-American disturbances.

"In the face of an accomplished situation such as the one in which we find ourselves, the sane, the logical, the humanitarian thing is to find formulas which will permit us to correct the errors and to help a long-suffering people to find the path to liberty."

Ambassador Facio supported the call for creation of an inter-American defense force. He declared: "If we accept the thesis that there be created an O.A.S. military and police force . . . not only will there have been corrected the unilateral action which the United States government believed itself obligated to take while the O.A.S. did not act, but also the inter-American system will be strengthened and the Dominican people will be helped to find a democratic exit from the tragedy which they are undergoing. With the presence of an O.A.S. force guaranteeing peace and order, it will not be difficult to achieve the formation of a Dominican government of national unity."

The speech by the able Costa Rican ambassador marked a turning point in the debate at the O.A.S. Further impetus for the creation of an inter-American force came in a message from the O.A.S. committee in Santo Domingo, which stated: "We consider that it would be useful, in order to aid in bringing a return of the Dominican situation to normalcy, for the member states that are in a position to do so to establish a combined inter-American military force under the Organization of American States to achieve the objectives that are set by the meeting of consultation." Ambassador Bunker warned the delegates: ". . . It seems to me, Mr. Chairman, that time is running out . . . We are faced with a practical, urgent situation . . ."

In the early morning hours of May 6 a vote was finally taken. The minutes of the meeting laconically report this notable occasion:

PRESIDENT: Those in favor will please raise their hands, showing their acceptance of the project.
SECRETARY: Fourteen votes in favor.
PRESIDENT: Votes against?
SECRETARY: Five votes against.
PRESIDENT: Abstentions?
SECRETARY: One abstention.
PRESIDENT: The Tenth Meeting of Consultation of Ministers of Foreign Relations has approved the project by 14 votes in favor, five votes against and one abstention.

Chile, Ecuador, Mexico, Peru, and Uruguay had cast their votes against the resolution. The Venezuelan delegate, who had abstained, declared that his country now believed that "the period of just criticisms has ended, in order to begin constructive and democratic action."

The historic resolution noted that—

"The formation of an inter-American force will signify *ipso facto* the transformation of the forces presently in Dominican territory into another force that will not be that of one state or of a group of states but that of the Organization of American States, which organization is charged with the responsibility of interpreting the democratic will of its members;

"The American states being under the obligation to provide reciprocal assistance to each other, the Organization is under greater obligation to safeguard the principles of the Charter and to do everything possible so that in situations such as that prevailing in the Dominican Republic appropriate measures may be taken leading to the reestablishment of peace and normal democratic conditions."

Therefore, the meeting resolved—

"To request governments of member states that are willing and capable of doing so to make contingents of their land, naval, air or police forces available to the Organization of American States, within their capabilities and to the extent they can do so, to form an inter-American force that will operate under the authority of this Tenth Meeting of Consultation.

"That this force will have as its sole purpose, in a spirit of democratic impartiality, that of cooperating in the restoration of normal conditions in the Dominican Republic, in maintaining the security of its inhabitants and the inviolability of human rights, and in the establishment of an atmosphere of peace and conciliation that will permit the functioning of democratic institutions.

"To request the commanders of the contingents of forces that make up this force to work out directly among themselves and with a committee of this meeting the technical measures necessary to establish a Unified Command of the Organization of American States for the coordinated and effective action of the Inter-American Armed Force. In the composition of this force, an effort will be made to see that the national contingents shall be progressively equalized. . . .

"That the withdrawal of the Inter-American Force from the Dominican Republic shall be determined by this meeting."

On May 7 the O.A.S. five-man committee that had been sent to the Dominican Republic submitted its first report. This detailed the committee's work, particularly its efforts to secure a ceasefire, efforts which culminated in the signing of the "Act of Santo Domingo."

The committee provided a description, too, of what it found when it flew to Santo Domingo: "From the moment it arrived in Santo Domingo, the special committee was deeply moved and saddened at the sight of this country on a war footing. Stores were closed, including those selling foods and other necessities. Also closed were banks and government offices; and in general, the city's entire normal activity had come to a halt. Many refugees and other persons were in asylum in the embassies of the various American countries, and the chiefs of mission of these countries personally told us that they were concerned that there were no guarantees for the premises of their respective missions. Consequently, there was an evident lack of security and of authorities having effective control of the situation. Public services were non-existent, including the most essential ones of water, electricity and telephones. The atmosphere was one of tragedy, mourning, and real human anguish. Rumors and other unverifiable reports were circulated regarding bloody incidents in various parts of the city."

The committee reported on its conferences with both Dominican factions. At Caamaño's headquarters a curious incident was noted:

"The special committee was witness during that [May 3] interview with the so-called 'Constitutional Military Command' to one detail that could not pass unnoticed. This was the presence of a uniformed person carrying arms, who said he was part of the Command and who spoke Spanish with a pronounced foreign accent. The secretary-general of the Organization of American States interrogated him in a loud voice before everyone, asking him: 'Who are you? What are you doing here?' The person replied: 'I am André Rivière, my nationality is French, I fought in the French army in Indochina, and I am working in Santo Domingo. I have joined this Command.' While he took no part in the conversations, Rivière was in the discussion room during the time of the interview, and the authority with which he gave orders to the guards posted at the windows and the door where we were was quite obvious. Some information obtained later regarding this soldier was to the effect that he was an instructor of frogmen who had arrived in Santo Domingo during the Trujillo regime."

The committee interviewed the members of the military junta which was then in power, and it questioned the junta regarding the background of the U.S. military move into the country. The committee thus obtained a copy of the historic note from Colonel Pedro Bartolomé Benoit, president of the junta, to U.S. Ambassador Bennett which led to the landing of American forces. The committee's report stated:

"Colonel Benoit explained that the deterioration of public order in the city of Santo Domingo, which started on the day that the movement against Sr. Reid Cabral began, and the conditions of anarchy and complete disorder that prevailed in the capital of the country had led him to request the aid of United States armed forces in order to give protection to the diplomatic missions and foreign persons and entities in general. Colonel Benoit added that he had received an urgent request from the diplomatic missions for protection that he was not able to provide.

"Colonel Benoit also stated that the request had been made to the United States in a note, a copy of which was transmitted later to the special committee, which read literally and in full, as follows:

SEAL OF THE DOMINICAN REPUBLIC
DOMINICAN REPUBLIC
DOMINICAN AIR FORCE
OFFICE OF THE CHIEF OF STAFF
"19TH OF NOVEMBER" AIR BASE
SAN ISIDRO, NATIONAL DISTRICT

April 28, 1965

The Ambassador of the United States
United States Embassy
Santo Domingo

Dear Mr. Ambassador:

Regarding my earlier request I wish to add that American lives are in danger and conditions of public disorder make it impossible to provide adequate protection. I therefore ask you for temporary intervention and assistance in restoring order in this country.

Truly yours,
Pedro Bartolome Benoit
Colonel
President of the Military Junta
of the Government of the Dominican Republic

The committee summed up its accomplishments: "The special committee achieved, under truly dramatic circumstances, the main objectives set forth in the previously mentioned resolution with respect to ceasefire, the orderly evacuation of persons who had taken asylum or refuge, and humanitarian assistance to the Dominican people without any distinction as to parties or conflicting factions. The special committee also achieved the demarcation of a safety zone in the city of Santo Domingo in accordance with the map officially drawn up by its military advisors. This map was transmitted to both parties . . .

". . . The Act of Santo Domingo and the results thus far obtained by the special committee constitute the first state of a process of restoring peace and normality in the Dominican Republic . . ."

Despite this hopeful note, the situation in Santo Domingo did not improve. The committee continued its efforts to achieve peace and normalcy, but the frustrations were many. In a second report, submitted May 19, the committee provided an insight into the obstacles that it continually encountered:

". . . [There have been] many and increasing denunciations by both parties of violations of the ceasefire and of the Act of Santo Domingo . . . A report of the incidents in various parts of Santo Domingo, which have involved the parties and which have flagrantly disturbed the ceasefire agreement, would be almost endless. . . .

"The special committee was able to appreciate the seriousness of the radio broadcasts by both parties, which frequently contained inflammatory remarks. On May 14, 1965, upon repeating to the parties that it was imperative that they conform strictly to the ceasefire, the special committee requested both Colonel Caamaño and General Imbert to allow the O.A.S. to control the radio broadcasting.

"This plea to the parties to accede to essential cooperation in this field was formally made by the special committee during the interviews held on May 14, 1965. Unfortunately, it did not produce the desired results, for whereas General Imbert promised to place the radio of San Isidro under the control of the O.A.S., as requested, Colonel Caamaño said that he would accept only an agreement that would cover specified topics to be excluded from radio broadcasts, but that he would not agree to international control by the O.A.S. Since one party made this exception, it was impossible to reach an agreement on this very fundamental matter.

"The special committee spared no effort to obtain a meeting between the heads of the two conflicting factions, Colonel Caamaño and General Imbert. It was hopeful that the achievement of such a meeting might help to iron out differences . . . To this end, the special committee held conversations on May 12, 1965, with General Imbert and Colonel Caamaño and gained a categoric promise from General Imbert to be willing to meet with Colonel Caamaño. Colonel Caamaño, for his part, refused such a meeting, but after repeated and substantiated requests from the committee . . . Colonel Caamaño agreed to meet with General Imbert. Under these circumstances, after holding a conversation outside the office where we were, on a subject unknown to us, Colonel Caamaño returned to our discussion table and said that, before talking to General Imbert, he would like a meeting to be held between a representative of his and one of the other party, in order to agree upon details of the interview. He also said that he would appoint a vice minister for this purpose. . . . It was agreed that this meeting would be held in the papal nunciature the next morning at 10:00 A.M. and that the committee would attend. . . .

"[General Imbert agreed to this arrangement and] on the day and the hour previously indicated, the special committee went to the nunciature, where it found Sr. Federico Infante Caamaño, representative of General Imbert. At that time, the papal nuncio told that committee that, as had been agreed, he had gone to the offices of Colonel Caamaño to bring the vice minister who was to represent him in these conversations; however, it had been impossible to do this, because Colonel

Caamaño said that first he wanted to read the minutes of the session of the Meeting of Consultation in which the committee presented its first report. . . .

". . . [The committee agreed to provide a copy of the minutes and then] asked Colonel Caamaño if his representative would attend the meeting previously agreed to, and he replied that this would be impossible, in view of the attacks upon his forces by United States Marines in Vicente López and Caracas Streets. . . . The committee then proceeded immediately to determine what had happened, and through the United States embassy was able to ascertain that unfortunately there had been an incident in the place mentioned by Colonel Caamaño, but that the Marines had already withdrawn and firing in that sector had ceased."

Later in the day, still another incident prevented a meeting of the rebel and government representatives: ". . . The committee, from its location at that moment in the papal nunciature, heard violent firing and we saw that units of the Dominican military air force were making flights over the city . . . The result of those flights was the downing of one of those aircraft, caused by fire by United States forces, and at the same time, the silencing of the [rebel-operated] Santo Domingo Radio and Television station."

The O.A.S. committee never did succeed in getting representatives of the warring groups to sit down together at a conference table.

Official reports, by their very nature, are usually

coldly unemotional. Having presented their first report on May 7, the members of the committee submitted to questioning by other O.A.S. delegates. In answering these questions at a closed session, the committee members provided personal and dramatic accounts of what they had seen.

At one point the Uruguayan delegate requested, ". . . I should like to ask the committee if it is of the opinion . . . that the situation in the Dominican Republic constitutes a threat to the peace and security of the Hemisphere?"

Colombia's delegate, Alfredo Vázquez Carrizosa, replied: "Is the situation such that it can endanger peace and security? My reply is yes. Yes, there is a situation that endangers peace and security.

"The reasons are very clear. A disturbance or even a guerrilla action in a member state where the elements of order and constituted authorities exist is not the same as in a state where the absence of the state is noted, evaluated and recorded. What is to be done, Sr. Delegate, in the absence of the state? What does the system do when the state does not exist? What happens when blood is running in the streets? What happens, Sr. Delegate, when an American country—and I am going to speak quite frankly so that you may think about this with all the perspicacity we know you to have—is, under these conditions, in the neighborhood of Cuba? Do we sit on the balcony to watch the end of the tragedy? Do we all sit down as if we were at a bullfight waiting for the crew to come? What are we to do, Sr. Delegate?

"We are in a struggle against international Communism; and we are in a world, Sr. Delegate, in which America is not even separated from the other continents, even by the ocean. We form part of the world and we form part of the conditions existing in the world. The Dominican Republic, like any other country in the Americas, is a part of the system, and it is the system that will suffer from the lack of a head of state in any of its members. . . .

"The problem is one of deep political meaning, of profound significance, of Hemisphere importance much more serious than any of the other American revolutions could be. There have been many revolutions in America. There have been revolutions in my country; there have been some, I believe, in yours, and I do not believe that a revolution in itself justifies the intervention of the inter-American system. . . .

"[But] what are we to do, Sr. Delegate, when, as the report states, the president of a junta says, 'I cannot maintain order with respect to the diplomatic missions?' And what are we to do, Sr. Delegate, when that chief presents a note in which he requests the assistance of another country and confesses with the sincerity that we have heard, 'Gentlemen of the special committee, the diplomatic representatives asked me for protection and I did not have the elements with which to protect them.'"

Guatemala's delegate, Carlos García Bauer, also replied to the Uruguayan representative. He said: ". . . We in the committee often asked ourselves and commented on the advisability of having all of the members of this meeting visit the Dominican Republic in order to see, on the scene of events itself, the situation prevailing in that country: in a state of war, when we arrived, without water, without lights, without telephones, without public services. The lobby of the very hotel where we stayed was a scene of war: children and women sleeping in the lobby itself.

"The diplomatic corps, which met with us, also told us of the serious situation which they had gone through and were going through; anarchy ruled; the attacks that the diplomatic missions themselves had suffered; the wounded . . .

". . . Although there are those who proclaim that they represent authority in each sector . . . nevertheless it can be seen that they have no absolute control over the situation when the spectacle of wounded and dead persons is seen. We asked how many had died, how many had been wounded, and I believe that I can say . . . that at least 1500 persons have died in Santo Domingo."

The committee members were also questioned about Communist infiltration in the rebel movement. To this the Colombian delegate replied: ". . . Many delegates accredited in the Dominican Republic, and I can include my country's diplomatic representative, feel that, if not Colonel Francisco Caamaño, whom I do not know to be personally a Communist, there are indeed numerous persons on his side that, if they are not members of the Communist Party, are actively in favor of Fidel Castro's system of government or political purposes." Similar statements were made by other members of the committee.

On May 12 the Honduran government notified the O.A.S. that it was making available an army contingent as its contribution to the inter-American military force. The Honduran delegate declared, "The government of Honduras believes that the American states are obliged to give each other reciprocal assistance . . ." Nicaragua and Costa Rica also promised to send units.

The Honduran troops were the first to arrive in Santo Domingo. Two hundred and fifty soldiers were flown on May 14 to San Isidro in transport planes, and from there taken to an encampment. The next to arrive were twenty Costa Rican military policemen and 164 Nicaraguan soldiers. Tiny El Salvador placed at the disposal of the O.A.S. three Salvadorian military staff officers.

On May 21 Brazil announced that it was contributing 1250 men to the inter-American force. The Brazilian contingent would include an infantry battalion, a police platoon, a logistic support group and a company of navy riflemen. Ambassador Bunker announced that as soon as the Brazilian units had arrived in the Dominican Republic, the United States would withdraw a number of troops equal to the number of the total Latin American contingent —approximately 1700 men. (Ambassador Bunker on May 22 put the U.S. total at 14,400 men in Army units, 6100 in a Marine brigade, and 1000 in Air

Force support units. All of these were offered as part of the inter-American force.)

On May 22 the O.A.S. adopted a resolution requesting "the government of Brazil to designate the commander of the Inter-American Armed Force and the government of the United States to designate the deputy commander of that force." Brazil selected Lieutenant General Hugo Penasco Alvim, a veteran of the Brazilian Expeditionary Force that fought in Italy in World War II, as the commander of the Inter-American Force. Selected to be the deputy commander was Lieutenant General Bruce Palmer, Jr., commander of U.S. forces in the Dominican Republic.

On May 23, 1965 a historic document was signed in Santo Domingo by O.A.S. Secretary-General José A. Mora and the commanders of the American, Brazilian, Costa Rican, Honduran, and Nicaraguan forces. The document stated:

1. The Inter-American Force is hereby established as a Force of the Organization of American States.

2. The Inter-American Force shall consist of the Unified Command and the national contingents of member states assigned to it.

3. The Unified Command shall consist of the Commander of the Inter-American Force, the Deputy Commander and the Staff.

4. The Commander of the Inter-American Force shall exercise operational control over all elements of the Force. He shall be responsible for the performance of all functions assigned to the Force by the Organization of American States and for deployment and assignment of the units of the Force.

5. Members of the Force shall remain in their respective national services. During the period of assignment to the Force, they shall, however, serve under the authority of the Organization of American States and subject to the instructions of the Commander through the chain of command. Command of national contingents, less operational control, shall remain vested in the commanders of the respective national contingents.

The document noted that the Commander of the Force "will receive political guidance from the Meeting of Consultation."

For the Dominican people, this had been a time of tragedy.

For the United States, it had been a time of crisis.

For the Organization of American States, it was a moment of opportunity. The Organization represents twenty independent countries, each with its own heritage, outlook and traditions. Despite these divergencies, and despite some hesitation and some acrimony, the O.A.S. did seize the opportunity that was offered, and in so doing it also made history. Step by step the O.A.S. asserted itself with greater authority, and these steps culminated in the establishment of the Inter-American Force.

With the arrival of the Brazilian troops, the United States began pulling out some of its forces. By the first week of June, the last of the U.S. Marine contingent boarded its ships, leaving behind only U.S. Airborne and Air Force units. These were part of the Inter-American Force. Brazilian General Alvim arrived, and he assumed command of the Force. The troops of various nations painted

"O E A" (O.A.S.) on their helmets, and joint jeep patrols began driving through the International Zone.

The O.A.S. took on greater responsibilities. The National Palace, held by loyalist troops, formed an enclave within rebel territory, and had been the scene of heavy firing and sniping. In order to end this fighting, Brazilian troops encircled the palace, forming a buffer between the rebels and loyalists.

The O.A.S. took over the disbursement of U.S. aid funds, and O.A.S. officials worked to improve health conditions in both the rebel and loyalist areas. A three-man O.A.S. peace team, headed by Ambassador Bunker, flew to Santo Domingo and began to work for a political solution which would start the country on the road to peace and democracy once again.

25G